FISHING

FISHING

RICHARD ARNOLD

A PAN ORIGINAL

PAN BOOKS LTD · LONDON

First published 1967 by
PAN BOOKS LTD.,
33 Tothill Street, London, S.W.1

330 20203 0

2nd (revised) Printing 1970

*Printed in Great Britain by Richard Clay (The Chaucer Press), Ltd.,
Bungay, Suffolk*

TO MY WIFE

Contents

Illustrations in the Text

Chapter 1

INTRODUCTION

OF ALL sports practised in the British Isles, fishing has the greatest number of followers. Yet, in spite of this, there are more misconceptions about it than about any other sport.

The reason for this, I believe, is that there are so many different aspects of fishing. In my own case I have only to think of the word and a whole flood of different memories is aroused. Memories of days spent along the shoreline, sometimes with waves pounding in and beating against the rocks in angry spray; sometimes the sea rolling in gently – green and clear, on to a smooth beach. Perhaps I recall the steady plunge of a boat heading out to some distant mark or drifting across the rippled surface of a loch, and the thrill of the fish boring deep. I may think of the climb up some small, rushing burn, casting before me for those small, gallant fighters, the speckled trout; or of waiting for a float to dip and slide beneath the surface in the dark waters of a canal. I am fortunate, not because I am able to fish as often as I should like, for I am not, but because I get so much fun from it and because to me any form of fishing is better than none at all.

Most fishermen tend to specialize in only one branch of the sport, and even when discussing it, limit their conversation to one aspect. I know sea anglers who have never fished in fresh water, and vice versa. This is excusable because there are so many different branches of fishing, and an enthusiast in one is apt to forget those in which he does not participate. To one enthusiast, fishing may mean only coarse fishing; to another, sea fishing afloat; to yet another, especially to a Scot, only the pursuit of salmon.

The angler who can indulge in all branches of the sport is a rare creature. He must have plenty of time, and money, or be fortunate enough to be an angling journalist, travel agent, or in the tackle trade; and though he may fish for salmon, participate in match angling on some canal, or go afloat in pursuit of sea fish he will, in the end, gradually channel his skills and enthusiasms into one favourite branch of the sport.

Consider, for a moment, the different branches of fishing. There is, first of all, the distinction between sea fishing and freshwater fishing. Sea fishing is divided into afloat and ashore. Fishing afloat is subdivided into inshore fishing and deep sea fishing. Shore fishing is divided into beach, pier, or jetty, rock fishing and so forth. Even the sea fish themselves are divided into big game fish and ordinary fish.

Freshwater fishing is divided into two main groups. These are coarse fishing and game fishing – coarse fishing for such species as roach, rudd, pike, etc., and game fishing for salmon, sea-trout, and trout. The sport is again divided and subdivided into the style of fishing, e.g. fly fishing, spinning, legering; and also according to the type of waters fished, e.g. still waters, rivers, lochs.

Even if all this were not enough there are angling games in which tackle is used. Typical of these games are distance and accuracy casting competitions and tournaments, and though they form part of the angling scene they are none the less neither fishing nor angling. They approximate rather to 'skeet' and 'down-the-line' clay bird competitions in relation to the sport of field shooting.

At this stage let me point out that whereas all anglers are fishermen, there is often a distinction drawn between the two terms. Only anglers use a rod, line, and hook, but I always feel that the word 'fisherman' really refers to the person who nets, spears, or traps fish. However, when discussing the sport among anglers the term 'fisherman' may be used in a wider sense.

Angling, or fishing, is often described as a solitary sport. But the coach parties of anglers setting out on some long journey to a fishing match give the lie to this statement. The truth is that fishing may be pursued either alone, or in the company of others. It does not matter whether one is a millionaire or has only limited financial resources – the enjoyment, the fun, and the pleasure of it are there to be savoured. For angling demands little in return other than the observance of certain fundamental simple rules of sportsmanship and behaviour. Of course, to be able to indulge in certain types of fishing, especially trout and salmon fishing, one has to have plenty of money – but that is a question of property, not of the sport itself.

One of the charms of fishing is that it is never the same two days running. It continually presents different problems : problems connected with the ways and habits of the fishes, or the weather, or the state of the water, or the time of the year. Once the desire to fish has bitten the would-be fisherman, if he is of the right material he will pursue the sport all his life and no matter how experienced he may be, on each and every occasion or outing he will find himself learning new hints and tips. And despite what is written by the experts he will find he has many fishless days – fishless, but never 'empty' or 'blank'. A successful fisherman must be able to sum up weather conditions, the nature of the countryside, and a sense of the love of nature must be dominant in his makeup.

Observations at the waterside are part of the joy of fishing. The brilliant streak of a kingfisher, the antics of butterflies, scent and colour of flowers, tracks of creatures in the mud – all these prevent the day becoming a blank – fishless though it may be. In retrospect, fishing consists each day of an accumulation of incidents at the water's edge, not of merely catching, or not catching, a fish.

So much for fishing in general.

But what is angling? It is the pursuit of fish and involves the use of a rod, line, and hook which carries some form of bait or lure. Whether a small boy fishes for minnows with the legendary cotton, short stick, bent pin, and worm, or an affluent angler seeks tunny or shark equipped with stout rod and big reel, with harness and special chair, the principles are the same.

To fish successfully, the following basic rules should be observed :

1. Know the fish you are seeking in order that it may be correctly identified.

2. Know its habits, how, when and where it should be found.

3. Understand how to present a bait or lure to the fish, and when it should be used.

4. Know how to land the fish after it has succumbed to the lure.

Any good angler will also look at water and weather conditions and try to assess their effects on fish and aquatic life; try to imagine how, when and where the fish he is seeking would feed; discover how a fish would become alarmed and how it would react when hooked. From such an appreciation he can then go about the capture of his quarry.

Another fact to be learned is that with few exceptions, notably parts of the Thames, fishing in fresh water in Great Britain is rarely free and those who disregard this may find themselves in serious trouble for poaching. This could lead to criminal proceedings being taken resulting in the confiscation of equipment coupled with, perhaps, a fine and/or imprisonment.

Fishing in salt water is generally free, although certain estuarial waters may be privately owned. And so, despite the fact that fishing from boats may be legal, to fish from the shore may mean an act of trespass on or over a privately owned beach, foreshore, or salting.

Today, though this may be changed in years to come, most rivers in the United Kingdom are administered by River Authorities. These bodies have absolute authority over all waters in their area, including private lakes and ponds. To fish these waters, not only is permission required from the owners of the waters, but it is also necessary to hold a licence issued by the River Authority in question. Every river and water has its own permits and regulations which the angler has to observe.

The question of what equipment to purchase is obviously not best answered in the pages of a book. If the novice has an angling friend to help him he is fortunate. Otherwise he must go along to the tackle shop, place himself at the mercy of the salesman, and rig himself out with an outfit. If he is lucky he will have chosen a shop which has an experienced angler behind the counter, a man who knows local waters and understands the fishing conditions and is therefore able to advise the newcomer correctly on what articles of equipment to purchase. If he is unlucky enough to be attracted to a large departmental store, it is a fairly safe assumption that plenty of equipment will be sold to him, he will have a good deal less money in his pocket, and the fishing that follows will not be very successful.

Let us analyse these situations.

The knowledgeable friend: he will take the beginner to waters he knows, show him how, and what is even more important, why, certain tackle should be used for the fish which frequent that particular water. He will also show him how to present the lure or baited hook. He is using experience built around certain circumstances and the outfit selected in these circumstances is wisely chosen.

The local tackle dealer: with his expert knowledge he stands in very much the same position as the knowledgeable friend.

The department store assistant: working as a rule on salary and commission, in all probability he does not know, or even wish to know, the conditions under which the customer will be fishing. All he is interested in is selling tackle, and so, sell tackle he does.

Finally, there are many clubs and associations who will help the beginner along. Not only do many of these organize lectures and symposiums, but there is always someone to hand ready to give assistance in choosing the right tackle and the right way to use it. Some are run by works' organizations, some are merely little social clubs. For the freshwater angler, the various clubs and associations are often the only means by which the average working man can participate in the sport. Most waters are club owned or rented, and though day or visitors' tickets are often available, many clubs keep their waters strictly for members. For the man who is interested in competitive or match fishing, the club is the answer. But for the non-competitive angler, who shuns crowds and who likes to rove the waterside, the club of today will not be his social heaven. Most clubs prefer their members to fish matches regularly – and the solitary person who joins a club and then does not fish in matches will not remain very popular.

Through my own experiences, both practical and in the wholesale and retail tackle trades, I shall endeavour in the following pages to present the beginner with a general guide to all the various fishes to be caught, the habitats they frequent, and under each set of circumstances the tackle most suitable for successful fishing. In this way, by covering every aspect, the enthusiast in one branch may possibly be induced to take an interest in other entirely different facets of the sport.

There is only one other recommendation I can make to the newcomer: do not become so serious about it that all the enjoyment goes. Fishing is a sport, a recreation, and even though at times competition may enter into it, it should always be a delight and pleasure.

Part I

Fresh Water

COARSE FISHING

Chapter 2

COARSE FISH AND THEIR HABITATS

THE TERM 'coarse fishing' refers to the pursuit of fish in fresh water other than 'game fish'. The term 'game fish' refers to salmon, migratory trout, trout, char, and the grayling. The distinction arises from the spawning habits of the fish.

With the exception of the eel, spawning of coarse fish takes place in the spring months. This depends upon various conditions, such as temperature, and can vary from March to the end of May.

With the exception of the grayling, which spawns at the same time as coarse fish and is therefore classed with them, 'game fish' choose to spawn between October and January, according to the locality and meteorological conditions.

For coarse fish, from March 14th until June 16th, there is what is termed a 'close' season when one is not allowed to fish for them. The reason for this, of course, is to protect them during their spawning period.

There are, however, certain areas which do not apply the close season entirely. For instance, on the Broads there is an open break in the close season, and in Ireland there is no close season for coarse fish, resulting in numbers of English anglers travelling there each year. This has caused much heart-burning among anglers – some maintaining that a good sportsman would not want to fish during the spawning months anyway, and others that this attitude is hypocritical, that if it is legal to take fish in any place one should be able to take advantage of it. I am on the side of the conservationist and believe that a close period should be respected.

Though many freshwater fishermen bemoan the close season, chiefly on the grounds that they have to lay their rods aside for a while, they really have no sound reason for this attitude, for when the coarse fishing season ends game fishing is in full swing. Furthermore, as there is no close season for sea fishing there is absolutely no reason why the coarse fisherman cannot continue fishing throughout the whole year. Unfortunately many fishermen conceive prejudices about the branches of the sport in which they are not extreme enthusiasts, and such prejudices are difficult to dispel. To the game fisherman the idea of catching fish, weighing them, keeping them in nets for a while and then returning them to the water seems a little odd. To the fine fishing expert, the roach fisherman, sea fishing often appears to be crude and unskilled. The man who fishes still waters for fish weighing only a few ounces is looked upon with scorn by those who fish in the sea.

The keen angler will, in any case, make use of the close season to overhaul his tackle and equipment thoroughly, generally preparing for the opening of another season.

Which are the coarse fishes? They consist of different members of the carp family, the perch, the pike, and the eel. Plus, for reasons of spawning, the grayling.

There are about twenty different species of coarse fish commonly sought by the angler, and these are divided into the following main classes or families:

(a) *Percidae*, which includes the perch and the ruffe.

(b) *Cyprinidae* or carp family, which includes the carp, barbel, gudgeon, chub, tench, roach, minnow, stoneloach, bleak, and other popular sporting fish.

(c) *Esocidae*, or pike family.

(d) *Muraenidae*, or eels.

The largest of these families is that of the Cyprinidae, or carp family, and it is also a fairly safe assumption that the small roach is the most popular of all freshwater fish caught in Great Britain. Yet how many anglers think of the roach as a member of the carp family?

Before attempting to identify the various species of fish, an angler should know something about the anatomy and physical characteristics of a typical freshwater fish. In the accompanying sketch (Fig. 1) I have shown the main characteristics of a fish, but would point out that the specimen illustrated does not, in fact, exist in nature. Where a fish is described I have made reference to the various fins, the details of the number of rays to each fin, and other important factors, such as the number of scales along the lateral line, the coloration, shape, and approximate average weight.

In the fish illustrated (a) represents the gill cover, (b) a

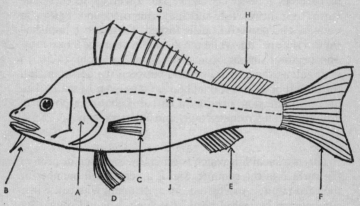

1 This shows the main physical features of most fish, though the specimen illustrated does not exist in nature

barbel, (c) the pectoral fin, (d) the pelvic fin, (e) the anal fin, (f) the caudal fin (or tail), (g) and (h) dorsal fins, and (j) the lateral line.

In the case of the caudal fin there are extra characteristics which aid in the identification of the fish. The end of it may be straight, forked, concave, or convex.

It is absolutely essential that an angler should be able to identify his fish. Even the beginner should be able to do this from his first outing, and though the following passages are a guide to the coarse fish likely to be caught, the beginner should supplement them by visits to museums and aquaria to see for himself what the fishes actually look like.

The following, in alphabetical order, are the freshwater fish most likely to be met with by the angler:

Barbel

This is a bottom-feeding fish. When hooked it puts up a powerful struggle and is a fast, tough fighter that has well earned its title, the 'Tiger of the Weir Pool'. General coloration – olive-bronze to olive-green body with a whitish belly and the fins sometimes coral tinted. There are four barbels, or barbules – hence its name. The lower lip recedes. The barbel is a heavy fish and may run to double figures in pounds. The powerful tail is forked. There are 5 branched rays in the anal fin, while the dorsal fin contains 8 or 9 rays. The pectoral fins are rounded. There are from 52 to 70 scales along the lateral line, and between the dorsal fin and the lateral line there should be 12, 13, or even 14 scales. The overall impression given by a barbel is that of a powerful fish with a long, rounded body and a flattish belly.

Bleak

This is a shoal fish which is generally found on or near to the surface in the summer, and is a very small member of the carp family. Apart from the matchman, who can win a competition by skilful bleak snatching, it is not sought by serious anglers. Some idea of its size may be given by the fact that one of the greatest competition anglers of all time, the late Jim Bazley, won a competition with 184 bleak, giving a total weight of 6 lb 12¾ oz. The record weight of this fish, caught on the Thames, was 3¼ oz. The bleak is very numerous in the Thames and Trent and can be a veritable nuisance by taking bait intended for other fish. On the other hand, it is a good fish to enter the youngster into the sport.

General coloration – the sides are silver with a greenish back, though occasionally the overall impression of this tiny and attractive fish is silver-blue. The body is slim. The lower jaw of the mouth projects. The long anal fin is concave, as also is the dorsal fin, which is short. The anal fin usually contains from 15 to 20 branched rays, while the dorsal holds 7 to 9. The tail is forked. Between the dorsal fin and lateral line there should be 7 to 9 scales, and scales along the lateral line should number from 46 to 54.

If fished for specially (and on occasions a keen competition angler will go all out for them), a slow sinking maggot or crysalid fished on or near the surface are good baits, and this fish calls for extremely quick striking.

Incidentally, bleak have a habit of worrying bread crust and other particles of food floating on the surface of the water, so a good method of getting rid of troublesome ones is to throw them a piece of bread or crust, which they will follow down the current, thus removing the shoal from your swim and enabling you to return to the business of angling for the larger fish.

Bream

A member of the carp family. There are two varieties of this species, the Bronze Bream, which is sometimes called the Common Bream, and the Silver Bream. Coloration – the Bronze Bream has a dark back with silvery-bronze sides and dark fins. The Silver Bream is lighter in colour but is, in fact, more green than silver. Both have the appearance of being hump-backed because they have narrow, flat bodies with very small heads. Of the two varieties the Bronze Bream grows to a larger size, the Silver Bream usually being weighed in ounces rather than pounds, although in small waters neither appear to attain any size. The Silver Bream can, like the bleak, sometimes become a nuisance to the serious fisherman.

Both species are to be found in lakes, still waters, and rivers, and when located are not very difficult to catch. They cannot, by any stretch of the imagination, be described as good fighters when on the hook, but they are popular because they enable anglers to make heavy baskets.

Bream is a bottom-feeding fish, and when caught exudes great quantities of slime. They are usually caught with bunches of maggots, bread flake, crust, paste, lobworms, cheese, and when bream are found it pays to use groundbait fairly generously.

In addition to the differences in size and colour, there are differences in scale counts. I have set out the characteristics of the two species as follows :

	Bronze or Common Bream	Silver Bream
Anal fin	Very long Concave	Very long Concave
Dorsal fin	Short, concave	Short, concave
Tail	Forked	Forked
Branched rays in anal fin	7 to 9	19 to 24
Branched rays in dorsal fin	8 to 10	7 to 9
Lateral line	49 to 57 scales	44 to 50 scales
Lateral line to dorsal fin	11 to 15 scales	8 to 11 scales
Record weight	13½ lb	4½ lb

Carp

There are four kinds of carp to be caught in British waters – the Common Carp, the Mirror Carp, the Leather Carp, and the Crucian Carp. Through the activities of Richard Walker and others who followed him, in recent times in this country carp catching has become recognized as a sport in its own right.

The most important variety in British waters is the Common Carp, which is the largest of the species and grows to an enormous size. The present record stands at 44 lb for a fish captured by Richard Walker in 1952, and at the time of writing this fish is still alive in the aquarium at Regent's Park Zoo, London, to which it was presented.

A characteristic of the Common Carp is the short, deep, and thick body. The mouth has thick, projecting lips and has four barbels. Coloration – golden-brown shading to a yellowish-white towards the belly, with dark brown fins. The dorsal fin is very long and concave. The anal fin, also concave, is short. The thick tail is forked. The scales are large and there are usually from 34 to 40 along the lateral line. There should be from 5 to 7 scales between the dorsal fin and lateral line. There are usually 7 or 8 branched rays in the anal fin, and 17 to 22 in the dorsal fin. The long dorsal fin has 3 simple rays at the front, and there is a saw edge to the first one.

The Mirror Carp is a variation of the Common Carp, and can be identified by two rows of large scales along the lateral line and smaller scales along the base of the dorsal fin and near the tail.

The Leather Carp, another variation of the Common Carp, has, to all intents and purposes, no scales at all – usually only a few near the dorsal fin.

Smaller than the other species, the Crucian Carp may be identified by the lack of barbels. Its fins are convex. The body is very short, deep, and flat, and it rarely weighs above 4 lb. There are also differences in scale counts. Along the lateral line there should be 28 to 35 scales, with 6 to 9 between the lateral line and the dorsal fin. There should be from 14 to 21 branched rays in the dorsal fin.

The carp is generally found in lakes, canals, ponds, and gravel pits, although occasionally they may be described as river fish and have been taken in the Thames and other big rivers.

Chub

This is a very timid fish, easily scared and put down by bank or boat noises. The chub is a river fish with a preference for fast- or medium-flowing waters. It is sturdy, with a thick body and large mouth. Coloration – a dark olive back with silvery sides, though as the fish grows older the silvery sides often tend to acquire a 'brassy' effect. The pelvic and anal fins are tinted with coral. The convex anal fin is an important feature in the identification of the chub as roach, dace, and rudd are close relatives and often confused with it by novices. These species all have concave anal fins. There should be from 7 to 9 branched rays in the anal fin and a similar number in the dorsal. Scale counts should show from 42 to 49 scales along the lateral line, with from 7 to 8 between the lateral line and dorsal fin.

A greedy feeder, the chub will take almost any bait which has been properly and carefully presented, putting up a powerful fight for a few moments after it has been hooked, a fight which soon tails off into a disappointing surrender. However, the chub can provide capital sport with the fly, and this is a branch of coarse fishing which is becoming more popular.

Dace

Like the bleak, this is a shoal fish and another member of the Cyprinidae. The body is long and slim and, unlike the chub, the head is not blunt and the mouth is smaller. Coloration – although the impression is that of a silver fish the back is fairly dark with greenish ventral fins which are sometimes, though not always, tinged with red. The short anal and dorsal fins are concave and should contain 7 to 9 branched rays in the former, and 7 to 8 in the latter. The tail is forked. There should be 47 to 54 scales along the lateral line and between the lateral line and dorsal fin 8 or 9 scales.

The dace is a widely distributed river fish, very plentiful in chalk streams. It is a good sporting fish for both summer and the winter and can provide the fly fisherman with much enjoyment. It is not a large fish and the fisherman who takes one in the region of 14 oz and upwards has cause to congratulate himself.

Dace feed upon insects both below and on the surface of the water, and though dapping the live insect is a profitable way of taking them they may be caught by legering with bread crust, particularly in the winter months. In fact, they may be caught at all depths of water. Oddly enough one does not encounter the odd dace on the feed – they seem to feed as a shoal and consequently one is apt to catch several at a time. The shoals have a habit of stopping feeding just as suddenly as they commence.

Eel

This is a good sporting fish provided that one discounts the small, immature bootlace creatures which pester the worm-fisher, swallow the hook, and make a tangle of the line. The average eel may weigh only a pound or two, but the British rod-caught record stands at $8\frac{1}{2}$ lb. They are to be found in most waters, including estuaries.

Grayling

This fish is often dealt with as a coarse fish but I prefer to give its characteristics under the section dealing with game fish.

Gudgeon

A splendid fighter, this fish is the miniature barbel, with a long, rounded body and a flattened belly. There are, however, only two barbels to its receding lower jaw. Both dorsal and anal fin are short and contain, respectively, 5 to 7 and 6 to 8 branched rays. Scale counts are 39 to 45 along the lateral line and 5 or 6 between the dorsal fin and lateral line. Coloration – dark brown with darker splotches on the sides. The length is about 6 to 7 ins., and with the record weight standing at $4\frac{1}{2}$ oz, even a 2 oz fish is rated as a good specimen. Apart from the fact that the gudgeon makes an excellent live bait, it also provides a really delicious meal.

Perch

This is often regarded as the most handsome of the fresh-water fish. A conspicuous feature is the humped back which is dark olive in hue, with sides of golden-greeny-brown shading towards white at the belly. Along the sides are six broad vertical black stripes which, like the stripes of the tiger, are part of nature's scheme of protective colouring, enabling it to remain almost invisible against a weedy background and serving a double purpose by protecting it from foes at the same time as hiding it from a potential victim. The pelvic and anal fins are red, and there are two dorsal fins, the front one being hard with sharp and spiky tips to the rays, which make considerable care necessary when handling the fish. The mouth of the perch is very large, the scales tough and small.

Many lakes and large waters hold considerable numbers of small, stunted perch which can be a nuisance to the angler, and a fish weighing over 1 lb is considered a good catch, although specimens of up to 4 or 5 lb are not uncommon. The perch is widely distributed and is to be found in canals, lakes, rivers, and ponds. As this fish is a predator and is to be found in areas where there are plenty of small fish and insects on which he can feed, a variety of methods are used for his capture. Methods such as float fishing with worms, gentles, and live minnows; spinning with dead natural bait or artificial lure; legering with worm or small dead bait, can all entice the perch to the basket.

Pike

The pike is the most voracious of all the British freshwater fish, feeding on almost anything. Young water fowl, frogs, fish, voles, and dead fish all form part of its diet. In fact, decomposing fish used as a legered bait makes an excellent lure for the big pike, and it is not surprising that it has earned the reputation of 'freshwater shark'. It is to be found in all kinds of waters ranging from still ponds to fast streams and rivers and, in particular, haunts reed-fringed margins of waters from the cover of which it can launch a swift and vicious attack on its quarry after a slow, careful stalk.

Its appearance, with long body, powerful tail, and sharp pointed nose – in fact almost a crocodile type snout – shows its fierce nature. The jaws bristle with sharp, pointed teeth which slope backwards, preventing the escape of anything taken between them. Owing to the dangerous teeth, the captured pike has to be handled with care, and a special tool known as a pike gag is used to keep the jaws open while the hook is being extracted. Even these pike gags do not always protect a fisherman's fingers or hands, for a large pike has been known to compress even the most powerful of them.

In colour the pike is olive green along the back with a white belly. There are vivid green markings and usually, though not always, creamy blotches along its sides. Apart from the dorsal fin, which is set well back, almost at the tail, the other fins are soft green in colour with dark irregular marks on them – again part of nature's camouflage scheme.

As a rule, the larger the water the larger the pike, and those taken from Irish loughs and Scottish lochs are usually much bigger fish than those caught in England.

As the fish grows to a good size it provides a sport which should satisfy the fisherman who enjoys a tussle. However, not everyone loves the pike. To trout fishermen he is a menace to be cleared from the water. To some coarse fishermen he is a pest who must be destroyed at all costs – certainly one would not want a pike in a hatcher. But it is a short-sighted policy to kill off pike on every occasion just because they consume an enormous quantity of fish as food which would otherwise give sport to the angler, for the main bulk of his diet is confined to the weak and sickly specimens which would not be worth catching anyway. One large pike is worth a hundred or so smaller fish, and though one generally finds fewer fish in pike waters their size is generally larger.

Pope (sometimes called the ruffe)

This is a similar fish to the perch, though very much smaller. It has not as wide a distribution as the perch, but is often mistaken for one. The body is short and humped at the shoulder. There are two dorsal fins, the front one having spiky rays, and these fins are a good identification point, for whereas the dorsal fins are separate in the perch, in the pope they are joined together.

The pope rarely reaches a weight of more than 5 or 6 oz but, in spite of its size, it has a large mouth and is a greedy feeder and, unless specially fished for, can become a nuisance.

Roach

Here is the reason for fishing for the great majority of British freshwater fishermen, and it is safe to say more small roach are caught in fresh water in Great Britain than any other fish. When it comes to a fish weighing over $1\frac{1}{2}$ lb, the position is different and it is the ambition of most roach fishermen to land specimens over 2 lb in weight.

It is a graceful fish with a shapely, though thick-set body, with a small head. The eyes and fins are red, the back is olive or dark green, the sides are a striking silver and the belly is whitish in colour. The anal and dorsal fins are concave, the latter set fairly well forward above the pelvic fins. There are from 9 to 12 branched rays in the anal fin and from 9 to 11 in the dorsal fin. There should be from 40 to 46 scales along the lateral line, and 7 to 9 between the lateral line and dorsal fin.

Hybrids, the result of crossing between roach and other fish, are likely to cause trouble in identification because there are roach-bream and roach-rudd hybrids. The hybrid roach-bream is fairly easy to identify, but the identification of the roach-rudd can pose something of a problem. In the roach the lower lip to the mouth recedes, while in the rudd it projects. This feature, together with the scale counts, should (and I write *should* because the matter is not at all simple) assist the angler to identify the fish properly.

Because the roach is the fish most often caught by anglers it has become very wary, particularly the larger one. On waters which are hard-fished, very fine tackle is essential, and it is the pursuit of fish in these circumstances that confirms the view that roach fishing is an art.

The most general bait used for roach fishing is the maggot (or gentle), but other popular baits are freshwater shrimp, hemp seed, bread flake, paste, crust, cheese, wasp grub, lobworm, and stewed wheat, and on the Continent large roach are often caught by spinning.

Rudd

As has been stated, this fish is very similar to the roach and does inter-breed with it on occasions. It differs from the roach in that the dorsal fin is set more towards the tail, and though they are both silvery fishes, the rudd carries golden tints along its olive-green back and its sides are silvery-blue. All the fins are usually red and much less concave than those of the roach. There are 10 to 13 branched rays in the anal fin and 8 to 10 in the dorsal fin. There should be from 39 to 44 scales along the lateral line, and between the lateral line and the dorsal fin there should be 7 or 8.

Particularly active during the summer months, the rudd is a shoal fish regarded chiefly as a surface feeder. However, it also feeds in mid-water, and several large-sized specimens have been recorded as caught when bottom fishing. Though it is found in some rivers, in the main it may be described as a fish of still, or very slow-moving waters. In addition to the usual coarse fishing methods, using leger and float, the rudd gives excellent sport to the fly fisherman, and flies dressed to represent white moths and fished at dusk are a very effective bait.

Tench

This fish has similar habits to the bream and is often found in waters holding the latter. It likes still waters, particularly muddy-bottomed lakes and ponds, where it grubs about among the roots of weeds so that its presence is often betrayed to the angler by streams of air bubbles rising to the surface. Areas of soft weed are its favourite haunt and on hot summer days it is to be found in the shade of large lily leaves or in the marginal rushes of the water. Although the tench is a warm month fish and winter angling for them is rarely successful, a warm, still, unseasonable winter's day may bring them on the feed.

The tench is a handsome fish with a short, deep body,

varying in colour, according to the water from which it is taken, from olive green to amber. The eyes are red, and there are two small barbels at the mouth. All the fins, which are black, are convex, and the tail is rounded. The anal fin should hold 6 to 8 branched rays, while there are 8 to 10 in the dorsal fin. The scale count should show from 39 to 44 along the lateral line and 7 or 8 between the lateral line and the dorsal fin.

Very tenacious of life, the tench is well covered with slime and puts up a good fight, in spite of his sluggish nature, when hooked. The most popular methods of tench fishing are legering with large baits, especially in deep water, and float fishing with a very lightly shotted float.

*   *   *

The foregoing are brief notes on the various species of coarse fish which the angler is likely to catch. There are other, rarer species such as the burbot, but one is not likely to encounter them unless fishing in a favoured locality. The *Char*, which is a member of the salmon family, is dealt with in the game fishing section of this book. The *Smelt* and the *Flounder*, which are both taken in river estuaries and in brackish water, are essentially salt-water fish and are dealt with under the section dealing with sea fishing.

The beginner will, of course, need to know where the fishes described are likely to be found. For angling purposes, waters are divided into different categories: still, medium and slow moving, fast rivers and streams.

Still water: Carp, tench, perch, bream, roach, rudd, chub (sometimes), pike, eel.

Medium and slow moving water: Roach, rudd, chub, dace, bream, carp, perch, pike, eel, bleak, gudgeon.

Fast moving rivers and streams: Barbel, chub, dace, perch, bleak, gudgeon, eel.

Chapter 3

FLOAT FISHING

FLOAT FISHING is the angling technique most commonly seen on inland waters. Contrary to popular opinion, the float is not employed solely as a bite detector but has, in fact, several rôles to play.

The float may be employed to manoeuvre or 'swim' a baited hook into some place into which the angler is unable to cast directly. It may be used to swim the lure a considerable distance downstream. This method is known as '*trotting*'. Alternatively, the float may be used merely as a means of keeping a baited hook off the bottom, or above a bed of weeds, or maintaining the lure at some predetermined depth.

Again, floats may be used in combination with other methods, e.g. as a bite detector and at the same time to 'trot' the lure downstream and then hold it at a predetermined depth.

Floats, which are manufactured from many different materials, are made in a great variety of size, style, and colour. They are, in fact, very attractive items of angling equipment which often tempt an angler into their purchase whether he needs them or not. I know several anglers who have extremely good and varied collections of floats which have never been used, and they still go on acquiring more and more.

Two considerations apply when selecting a float. Firstly, what type of water is going to be fished? and secondly, what is going to be the weight of the baited hook, coupled with the strength and weight of line used?

Rough or fast flowing waters require a larger or heavier float than softly flowing waters, or still waters. Under these conditions (I here refer to fast moving waters) a lot of weight is required to get the bait near the bottom. In still waters a very light float which balances the weight of the baited hook, without the addition of any other form of weight, might be sufficient.

The wise fisherman therefore comes to terms with this problem and selects the smallest, lightest float he can use for the job in hand, carefully weighing up water conditions, wind conditions, weight of line, weight of sinker, the type of fish angled for, and the weight of bait and hook.

The float selected should slide under the surface of the water (or dip) when even the lightest of bites is made. It should not have much air resistance when it is cast, and at the same time must disturb the water surface as little as possible when hitting it.

The beginner is advised to purchase his floats in three different sizes, namely, light, medium, and heavy, to enable him to match his tackle to conditions prevailing on his fishing days.

It is essential that the float possesses the correct colour. Two factors arise here. The side which is below the surface of the water must appear to the fish as something which is naturally upon the water : however, the portion of the float which is above the surface must be bright and conspicuous to the angler. The undersides of floats are often white, to match in with the surface as seen from below, sometimes being painted a dark green or brown, to give the appearance of wood or leaves which are on the water surface. For float tips the best colours are bright orange, yellow, or red. Modern fluorescent paints are excellent for this purpose, and are easily obtainable from tackle shops so that the angler may touch up the floats to suit his own taste.

There are many different types of float on the market.

Celluloid floats are popular. They are inexpensive to buy, light to carry, and can usually be loaded with a fair number of shot. This is very important in moving water. They also have the advantage that they are damp-proof and they keep a clean appearance. Painted floats, from balsa wood for instance, have to be continually touched-up and repainted. Celluloid floats are made in different designs and are a fairly 'safe' purchase by a beginner. The best size of celluloid float to buy is that in the 'medium' weight range.

Quill floats are popular and mainly used for light angling. They are manufactured from the quills of crows, geese, turkeys, and porcupines. Turkey and goose quill floats are usually from 4 to 7 in. in length whereas the porcupine quill may vary from 3 to 10 in. in length.

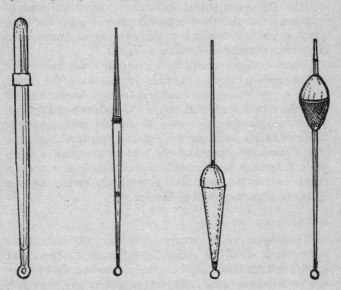

2 Types of floats: (*left to right*) celluloid, quill, antenna, chub

Cork floats provide the greatest varieties in styles, shapes, and sizes. They may range from a tiny float used for chub fishing, up to a pike or carp float of considerable size. It is among the cork floats that the heavy-duty type of float is found.

Types of celluloid, quill, and cork floats are shown in Fig. 2.

Of the types of float encountered by the angler I think

that the antenna type requires special mention. As the title indicates this float has a long, slender antenna extending from the cap. This offers little or no wind resistance and is coloured so that it remains visible to the angler when the remainder of the float is below the surface. The antenna float is very suitable for windy days when the surface of the water is rough. However, the beginner must not fall into the trap of purchasing his antenna float with an unduly long body. By the time sufficient shot or wire has been added to the float to sink it so that only the antenna shows, the wretched thing will sink completely!

The self-cocking type of float, generally made from celluloid or plastics, carries shot inside the float body. The angler may ring the changes on his floats and will usually end up by making his own to suit his own needs. For night fishing, of course, the float tips may be painted with luminous paint, or have a small piece of reflecting material, such as a 'paste' diamond, built into the cap on to which a torch beam is directed. Bubble floats, of which more later, are not really used as floats at all, but generally employed as a means of increasing casting distance.

Still Waters

While most canals may be classed as 'still' waters, together with small reservoirs, lakes, ponds, 'lodges', and pools, the term itself may be rather misleading. Still waters can vary from a canal 20 ft wide or a pond 20 or so yards across to a huge reservoir or lake of several thousand acres. Furthermore, especially on large lakes, there may be a current due to meteorological conditions, while even canals may have a slight current due to surge and flow from lock gates.

Bearing these remarks in mind, therefore, it follows that one cannot expect the same tackle to apply to all 'still' waters. If one is fishing from the bank or shore of a large pond or lake a rod, suitable for float fishing, would be from 9 to 11 ft in length. For fishing a narrow canal, a smaller rod, perhaps 8 ft in length, might be more suitable. But

36

again personal stature, height, strength of the angler all enter the picture.

Float tackle consists of rod, reel, line, trace, hooks, sinkers, and float.

Firstly – the rod. In materials for rod construction the angler has a wonderful choice. Cane, steel, alloys, Spanish reed, or glass-fibre, are all presented in bewildering array. By and large the action of a well-built cane rod, assembled by a master craftsman, cannot be beaten. But such a rod is very expensive. Some anglers and angling writers enthuse over Spanish reed rods. From my own experience in the tackle trade I would not accept one of these rods as a gift. Spanish reed really only owes its popularity to the fact that it is an extremely light material, and, when combined with a spliced-in built-cane tip, is a good match rod for the angler who is by nature a confirmed 'tiddler snatcher'.

I cannot think of a more outdated material for a rod than Spanish reed. Even the best of rods built from it are liable to split, and they should certainly never be used for any long casting.

Glass-fibre is a good material for rods. It has several opponents, who, as a rule, are on the side of the very best cane rods, who conveniently forget that not every one can afford to pay the price required: the family saloon car is very popular, but only a few can afford the expensive limousine. So too, the vast majority of anglers have to use 'bread-and-butter' rods. The modern glass-fibre rods, such as the 'tensilated' rods by Auger, give excellent service. They are light in weight, true in action, do not warp or take a set, and are not prone to accidental damage. In fact, for the average angler, who is probably unwittingly careless, glass-fibre rods are a boon as they will stand up to a terrific amount of rough treatment.

Built-cane rods are well and truly the best: provided one can afford them, and treats the rod properly, with care and affection.

However, the beginner must be fully conscious of the

fact that *there is no such thing as a general rod*. Each angling technique demands a special type of rod (Fig. 3).

Good American and Swedish rods on the market today, while suitable for game fishing and sea angling, are not suitable for the average British coarse fisherman. I once exported to the United States of America a set of English match and coarse fishing rods at the special request of an American manufacturer who wished to try and build them

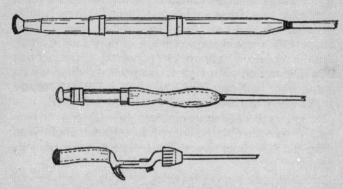

3 There is no such thing as the all-purpose rod. (*Upper*) Butt of bottom rod: similar butts are fitted to spinning rods. (*Centre*) Butt of fly rod. (*Bottom*) Butt, or offset handle, of bait casting or light spinning rod, Scandinavian or North American pattern

in his factory. Certainly he tried. He brought all his up-to-date equipment and resources to bear on the problem, but in the end, confessed he was licked. He just could not build a rod to suit British anglers and British conditions! I don't wish to state personal preferences, and when I mention names or types of rod I do not imply that they are best or that other makes are inferior : those named are merely used as examples. For carp fishing, of course, there is only one rod, that designed by Richard Walker, a specialist job built for a specialist purpose. The average angler might prefer pursuit of smaller quarry, small dace or roach being perhaps all he desires : a day on the river being his idea of fun, or a day on a gravel pit, without thought as to capture of large specimens.

For pleasure fishing, as opposed to competition fishing, a match rod is a wrong choice. The match rod has been specifically designed to have a very quick action tip, in order to obtain a fast strike. This has resulted in stiff, poor casting, poor playing rods. A stiff match rod is totally unsuited for casting long distances, especially with a fixed spool reel, and I would never recommend a match type rod for pleasure fishing.

It has always struck me as remarkable, when in the trade, the number of rods purchased by anglers, built to competition specifications, who do not intend to use them in matches at all. I was never, therefore, surprised to find how wrongly these anglers used their purchases.

Time after time match rods are returned to the makers. They are, of course, damaged, and accompanied by complaining letters. Spanish reed, in particular, seems to be the chief material about which complaints are made.

The fault lies in two places. Firstly, the salesman who sold the rod unsuitable for the purpose for which it was to be used (though this cannot always be helped, as for example, in the case of mail order business), and secondly the customer who purchased tackle not suitable for his type of angling.

The commonest cause of complaint was of damage to rods which snapped at a ferrule. Usually the complaint went something like this : 'I have only had the rod a couple of weeks, and on my second outing it snapped at the third cast. . .' Quite often, as the state of the rod indicated, it had been dreadfully used, and for some time too. But often enough such damage was genuine, generally brought about by an angler who tried to cast too heavy a weight too long a distance.

It stands to reason that for roach fishing, as for dace, perch, and so on, a rod need not be as substantial as that required for pike or carp. It seems to me to be ironical that

39

so many freshwater anglers refer to sea angling rods as 'telegraph poles' when, in actual fact, carp and pike rods for freshwater use are heavier, longer, stronger than light sea rods!

There is one rod, however, which I feel I must recommend. It is suited for both match and pleasure angling. The rod I refer to is known as the 'Swimversa' and it is a product of the old firm of Milwards Ltd. This firm, established as long ago as 1730, brought out this rod to try and defeat the bogies of poor casting and playing ability of the 'match' type of rod. In the 'Swimversa' the butt, which is of split cane, has a reverse taper under a long cork-covered handle. In short, the butt is finer in diameter than the top of the handle. This design has resulted in a rod with considerably increased casting power, particularly for double-handed casting. Morever, when the cast is completed and the rod held in the normal angling position, the slight reflex action in the butt coupled with the split cane top results in a very fast strike action.

The position of the reel on the butt varies the speed of the strike so that, using a 'Swimversa', the angler can literally adjust the 'strikeability' to suit the current angling conditions.

When comparing characteristics of match and general pleasure rods it should be remembered that the match rod has its action in the tip, whereas the pleasure rod should have the action lower down, resulting in better casting and playing properties.

Secondly – the reel. The type of reel used will depend upon the personal fad or preference of the angler, allied to the question of money available for the purchase of this article. By and large, however, for float fishing the fixed-spool reel (Fig. 4) is the most popular choice. It acquires its name from the fact that the reel does not turn, but the line is laid on to the spool through the medium of a pickup arm. To ensure uniformity of line over the spool surface the spool moves forward and backwards while the line is being picked up. The fixed-spool reel has two very great advantages over other types of reel in that it is easy to learn to handle, and it is capable of casting long distances. Fixed-spool reels may also be used with two or

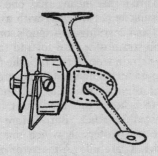

4 A fixed spool reel

more spare spools, each containing a different size of line. This is very useful as it enables an angler to switch over line strengths in but a fraction of the time it would take to wind off and re-wind on another line if using a centre-pin or a multiplier reel.

5 A centre-pin reel, now going out of fashion, except for fly-fishing

However, for 'trotting' and certainly for fly-fishing the centre-pin reel (Fig. 5) is the only possible choice, and for fishing fast water, as opposed to 'still' ones, this type of reel does carry advantages over other models. But the centre-pin does take longer to master, and I think that for the beginner the fixed-spool reel, such as the Intrepid 'Elite', would be the best choice.

Species found in still waters may range from small rudd to monstrous carp: this means that one rod or one reel would not be sufficient. However, with a reel such as the Intrepid 'Elite', and carrying two spools, one holding a line with a breaking strain of 4 to 6 lb, and the other holding line of breaking strain from 8 to 11 lb, the fisherman would find his reel requirements adequately covered.

The essential thing is that the rod and the reel must balance: and to achieve this they must be purchased together and tested together. But, before purchasing the equipment, the still waters in which one is going to fish must be considered carefully. A reservoir or gravel pit may be, to all intents and purposes, devoid of weeds. A private lake or pond may have very thick and strong weed growth and aquatic plants, not only in the centre, but fringing the edges. It follows, therefore, that where there is much plant life or weeds, a strong rod and line is required to deal with any heavy or powerful fish which is hooked and thereupon takes refuge in the tangle of plants.

Weed-free waters do not require so strong an outfit.

Furthermore, rods intended for fishing the larger species such as carp must be stronger than rods intended for roach and tench.

Thirdly – the line. There are two main types of fishing line in use today: monofilament and plaited. Here, I am referring only to lines for float fishing in still waters and not recognizing spinning or fly lines. The flax and cotton lines still on the market are reserved only for small boys.

Nylon or perlon monofilament lines give excellent casting range but, as their size increases, they become correspondingly springy. This is a great disadvantage as the loops which result have a tendency to catch round the spool, or the lower rod ring. If a very small diameter spool is used, the monofilament lines are apt to lie in springy coils over the water surface.

Plaited lines, on the other hand, do not come off the

spool in this manner and if the angler is going to use heavy lines then he should use these and not the monofilament type. If the angler is using two spools with a fixed-spool reel it is practical, however, to have a small capacity spool holding, say, 5 lb breaking strain line in monofil, and the larger spool holding the heavier line, say 11 lb breaking strain, in braided or plaited line.

The line must be treated carefully and though modern nylon and man-made fibre lines are waterproof, they should be taken off the reel spools and aired after each outing. The terminal portion should be examined carefully for signs of cutting or fraying, and knots scrutinized. Gravelly banks, sandy patches, debris on the bed of the water fished, all cut and weaken that portion of a line which is dragged over them: knots weaken the line: any one of these can result in a line snapping under the strain of a good strong fish, and the catch of a lifetime lost through sheer neglect on the angler's part in not caring for his line.

Fourthly – hooks. Hooks are frequently the subject of much discussion in the angling press. Much of the argument which is thus aired is given to the question of temper of the hooks, a considerable proportion of space is also given to sharpness of hooks. None of these discussions would ever take place if anglers would buy their hooks wisely. Cheap hooks are a false economy. The fisherman must, as a point of principle, always purchase the best hooks he can afford and, at this stage, let me add, entirely without any axe to grind, that the hooks marketed under the trade name of 'MUSTAD' cannot be bettered.

Hooks may be purchased loosely, or already tied or whipped to a nylon cast. It is advisable for the novice to purchase the hooks already so tied or whipped because not only does it eliminate the trouble of matching hook and cast together, i.e. ensuring that the right size of hook is attached to the right type of cast, but also eliminates the work in whipping the hook to the cast. This latter is a job which, if not done properly, means a lost fish almost as

43

soon as struck, certainly any fighting fish will be lost within seconds of the play beginning.

Too small a hook is a snare into which the beginner is tempted. Hooks are sized in different scales, but that known as the 'Redditch Scale' is the one most in use. In this scale the larger the number the smaller is the hook size. Thus a size 6 hook is bigger than a size 12.

For general float fishing the beginner will probably find that sizes 6 to 14 are best, but if fishing with hemp (which I will deal with later) then sizes 14 to 12 might be better. For pike, of course, larger hooks are used, but there are instances, when fishing for live bait for example, when very small hooks are the only effective size.

It is easy to be puzzled by the different hook patterns. The beginner is advised to specify 'Crystal bend' hooks, which is a very good type of hook for use against the smaller type of fish. I think, however, that to obtain a really first class hook, the 'Model Perfect' is the ideal type, particularly the fairly recently improved version.

Hook points must always be kept sharp and a small file is necessary to touch them up. Personally, I always discard the used hooks after a day's angling. Though they cost in the region of 6d. upwards each, they must be treated as expendable.

Fifthly – sinkers. Hook, line, and sinker are the tackle and though the sinker might seem a minor item, none the less it is an important portion of one's tackle. To get the bait down to the bottom and hold it there, or to cock a float correctly, some form of weight is required. Lead shot, lead weights, or lead wire are commonly used.

The commonest form of sinker for float fishing takes the form of 'split-shot'. This is so-called because it consists of lead pellets or shot which are cut down the centre. They are fastened on to the trace by nipping them together. These split shot are generally sold in dispensers or tins and range in size from very small pellets (similar to those found in shotgun cartridges) weighing from 200 to the ounce to what is termed 'swan shot', which is about the size of a currant.

44

Only through experience will the angler learn how many and of what size he should clip on to his tackle: but conditions of angling soon determine this.

Split shot are objectionable in that a clumsy angler, or one with cold or wet fingers, can damage the trace when trying to open up the slot to remove the pellet. Far better, in my experience, are lengths of fine lead wire. These can be wrapped round the trace without endangering its strength, for therein lies the weakness of the split shot as, if it is nipped on too tightly, it reduces the strength of the trace at that point.

In addition to shot or lead wire, what are termed 'half-moon' leads may be used. These are pressed together round the trace, but have the disadvantage that they are rather bulky and do set up air resistance when being cast.

The Technique of Float Fishing. So far we have dealt only with the equipment required – now we turn to the method.

Firstly, the approach to the waterside must be made quietly. Frightened fish mean no sport, and a noisy approach is the easiest way in which to frighten fish. Remember that it is not only your sport which is affected, anglers near your swim will also be prejudiced by your conduct. Clumping about on the bank soon puts fish down and renders them shy.

Likewise flashy clothing or equipment will also startle the fish. White shirts, made even whiter by proprietary soap powders, have no place at the waterside unless covered by more sober clothing. The angler's clothing should tone in with the background.

Tackle should be assembled away from the actual bank. It is absolutely useless going along to the bank, getting the tackle out, assembling it, throwing in groundbait and then hoping to catch fish. This is the best way to go about getting a fishless day. Every weekend I see similar actions along the Thames. Youths arrive riding cycles along the towpath, they clump about, pitching tents, and then settle down to fish, and invariably have a transistor radio with them.

Secondly, groundbait should be introduced to the water as soon as possible: preferably before assembling the tackle. A useful tip is to approach the swim carefully and bait quietly. The angler should then retire just as quietly, put his tackle up, and again cautiously approach the spot selected for fishing, ready to cast.

The purpose of groundbait is not to feed the fishes but merely to keep them interested. The best form of ground-bait for still water fishing is a light cloud bait. This can be purchased ready made up, and consists of a light crumby mixture. The purpose of a cloud bait is to act as an aperitif for the fish. It whets their appetites, but there is no satis-faction in it for them, so that the introduction of a larger piece of bait, on the hook, should seem more attractive.

But there is a danger in using too much groundbait. Plenty should be scattered at first. After that, just enough to keep the fish interested.

If one is using laying-on tactics the groundbait should be near the baited hook. This is best done by squeezing a lump of bait on to the lead itself. If using bread paste, a piece the size of a damson would be sufficient. Cloud bait is, of course, useless for this sort of angling.

At this point let me emphasize that the depth of the water must be ascertained. This is very important for unless this factor is known, and acted on, the day may well be lacking in sport.

To ascertain the depth use is made of what is termed a 'plummet'. This is a conical lead weight into the base of which is fixed a piece of cork (Fig. 6). Plummets for fresh-water angling are usually found in two sizes, $\frac{1}{2}$ oz and 1 oz. At the peak of the plummet there is a ring. Pass the hook through this and thrust the point into the cork in the base of the plummet. The plummet is then very gently lowered from the rod tip into the water until the bottom is found. With the plummet resting on the bottom and the line taut, the tip of the float should be level with the water surface. Having thus found the correct depth the angler can place the baited hook at the right depth over that portion of the water bed, and try to make contact with the fish.

In still water the float should be balanced with a sinker or lead shot so that the slightest touch of the bait by an interested fish will cause it to sink. To do this and ensure that the bait will sink slowly and naturally the weights should be placed as near the base of the float as possible. The bait being unweighted will sink in a natural manner. Quite often a fish will take such a slowly sinking offering.

6 Typical leads. (*Upper – left to right*) Arlesey bomb, drilled leger bullet, plummet. (*Lower – left to right*) paternoster, spiral, 'Capta'

In Fig. 7 the section A shows a simple float rig with three shot clipped on to the trace just below the float.

After casting the angler must so adjust his line that the float is just nicely cocked and balanced: a float which disappears is carrying too much weight, so that either the number of shot will have to be reduced or a larger float fitted, while the float which lies flat on the surface is not carrying enough weight and is also too high up the trace. By balancing the float so that it is poised in the water and with the line between float tip and rod tip as short as possible, the slightest tremor or movement when a fish moves the bait will be notified to the angler.

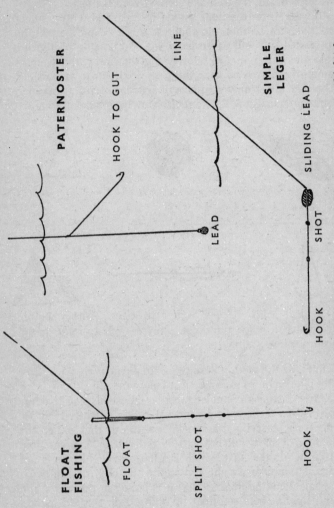

7. Types of terminal tackle. (*Left*) float tackle. (*Centre*) paternoster. (*Right*) leger

Laying-on is a term frequently encountered and is a form of float fishing. It differs from simple float fishing, however, by the fact that the lead used is very heavy, and the bait is anchored to the bottom. Hence the term 'laying on' (the bottom). The lead used in this form of fishing is that known as the 'leger' (Fig. 6). It may be spelled 'leger' or 'ledger' – either way is correct. A 'leger' weight has a hole drilled through the centre and may vary considerably in shape from round bullet, flat, piping, or coffin-shaped. The trace, or line, is threaded through the lead and a shot, larger in diameter than the hole through the 'leger', is pinched on to the trace about 6 to 9 in. above the hook. This prevents the 'leger' slipping down on to the hook.

After the depth has been ascertained through plumbing the measurement of depth is made from the lead to the tip of the float. This is done so that the baited hook will lie on the bottom. The line must be kept taut after the cast has been made and the float should incline at an angle of about 45° towards the angler.

Laying-on tactics should not be adopted if the bottom is thickly weeded or is covered with soft mud as, under either of these conditions, the bait would not be seen by the fish.

Weedy waters bring their own problems and one of these is to find the depth above a bed of them. If a plummet is used in the normal way it would, obviously, go straight through the weeds. Again, the use of a plummet might scare off the fish. By using a float, with a correctly shotted hook, tackle can be set up so that the baited hook will rest lightly on the top of the weeds.

First of all the tackle is set up in the normal way, but three split-shot are nipped on to the trace about 9 in. apart, the lowest about 6 in. above the hook. One tries to re-member the depth, or roughly estimate it, and then sets the float high enough up the running line so that, to all intents and purposes, the depth has been slightly overestimated. The line is then cast to the desired spot. If the float lies flat on the surface it means that it was set too high up the running line. This is because the shotted line is lying on the bottom and there is no weight hanging from the float. The float must therefore, between casts, be moved up and down the running line until finally it lies half-cocked. When this has been achieved the hook and the lowest split-shot are lying on the bottom, or on top of the weeds. If the float sits perfectly upright in the water, then it means that shots and hook are clear of the bottom.

When fishing still waters currents of air, gusts of wind, and so on may cause the float to swim or drag from its original position. Provided that the angler does not unduly disturb the water by continually recovering and recasting the line there is no objection to him doing this. Generally, however, the float moves with the wind and therefore in the direction in which bait falling on to the water would travel and is no disadvantage in the long run. A ripple on the water caused by wind is a good thing, it helps to put an opaque screen between fish and angler.

As the angler is concentrating his attention upon a float on the surface of water from which there may be a good deal of reflected light, it is suggested that he wear tinted glasses to prevent eye-strain and headaches. Continually peering on to sparkling water is a very tiring business.

Float Fishing in Moving Water. The basic principles are the same, though the applications vary a little. Firstly, in moving water more lead is required to get the bait to the bottom. The swifter the flow of current the heavier the lead required. If the current runs strongly, the best method is to place the shot, or lead wire, at intervals all along the trace to within a couple of inches of the hook-link.

Finding the correct depth at which to fish is not quite so easy in moving waters as in still waters. The portion which the angler fishes is called the 'swim' and this may well vary from a few inches in depth to several feet. It may, for example, be deeper at one end than the other, or, perhaps, deeper or shallower in the centre. The best plan is to try and adjust the float so that the bait just touches bottom at the deepest part.

Laying-on, as described earlier, can also be used in moving waters. It is, however, best to vary this technique by putting a single split-shot just above the hook-link, enough to balance a light float and yet sufficient to take the bait to the bottom. The cast should be made downstream and not across the current.

An excellent method of fishing with float tackle on moving waters is known as 'trotting'. This is usually done on swift moving waters and may be carried out either from bank or moored boat.

'Trotting' means letting the current carry the baited hook and float downstream, say, 20 to 30 yd. By this method the float is used as a means of exploring the waters. Plenty of groundbait is used for this method of angling and, as it is carried downstream, it is very important that the baited hook should follow the groundbait exactly.

The trace should be well shotted along its length when the trotting technique is used. I have mentioned earlier that for normal float fishing the fixed-spool reel is probably that mostly used; for trotting, however, the centre-pin reel proves itself to be the better model. Provided that the angler learns how to cast correctly with the centre-pin reel, a much more difficult art than when using a fixed-spool type, he will be able to double the number of casts per swim (when trotting) over his fixed-spool counterpart.

A variation of trotting is that known by the queer title of 'stret-pegging'. In this technique the float tackle is allowed to swim downstream, but it is held so that the float is stationary with the bait just waving off the bottom.

When trotting it is vital that the baited hook travels downstream *ahead* of the float. It is a common mistake, not always confined to beginners, to let the tackle swim downstream as soon as the float hits the water. When this happens it results in the baited hook dragging along the bottom in a very unnatural manner, and means that the angler is wasting his time as no fish will be attracted to it.

Additionally, the angler must learn to be in contact all the time by not allowing any slack line to fall on the water. If slack line is allowed to fall on to the surface it becomes impossible to strike quickly. The golden rule is that line from rod tip to float must always be tight enough to enable the angler to make a quick strike. If there is slack line on the water then the reaction time becomes far too long to be of any use to the angler.

The baited hook may be trotted quite a considerable distance. In a short 'swim' it is fairly easy to keep in contact all the time. All the angler has to do, in these circumstances, is to follow the line with the rod tip and then retrieve when the float has gone as far as the loose line allows. However, when trotting for some distance other factors have to be taken into account. First of all, monofilament line is rather elastic and the longer the amount of line out, then the greater it will stretch when a strike is made. There is thus an effective distance within which an angler can operate: beyond that distance the nature of the line will defeat him. Secondly, when trotting some distance it is difficult, unless one has a lot of experience, to pay the line out smoothly and, at the same time, keep the float and terminal tackle travelling down the river evenly.

After the cast has been made, therefore, the rod tip should be dropped until all slack line is taken up. Then, just a fraction of time before the float is checked, some line should be drawn off the reel and the rod tip raised. The extra line is thus drawn through the top ring and the line is kept taut. The same procedure is followed until the baited hook is as far down the current as the angler desires. Between paying out slack and lifting the rod tip the drill is to lower the rod tip at intervals and draw extra line from the reel. But the fisherman must beware of being caught out when doing this – he must be ready at all times to make a strike, and the line between rod tip and float must always be tight enough to allow him to do this.

It is sound practice to strike gently, by turning the wrist, at the end of each swim. Sometimes it pays the fisherman to deliberately break the rules and check the float at odd places during the swim downstream.

So far I have mentioned the fixed-spool reel and the

centre-pin for this type of angling. There is, however, another type of reel on the market which has a lot of advantages for all-round float fishing. This is the side-caster. This reel combines the rotating drum of the centre-pin with the ease of casting of the fixed-spool type. For casting, the drum is turned at right angles to the butt. After the cast has been made the drum is returned to its original, conventional centre-pin position. With the side-caster it is possible to make casts of considerable distance quite easily, while it retains the benefits of the centre-pin especially for big fish. This model of reel has received criticism that it will put a twist into the line. *Any reel will put a kink in any line!* The shape of the baited hook in water, revolving owing to the action of currents, or through being recovered, puts this twist into it. The judicious use of swivels and a centrally drilled bullet lead eliminates this twisting action, no matter what certain 'authorities' have implied.

Earlier in this chapter I have referred to the rôle of the float as a bite indicator.

The Float as a Bite Indicator. It has often been assumed that a movement of the float, other than that made by wind, or drag of debris against the line, means that a fish has taken the baited hook. There is much more to it than that. In nine cases out of ten it is possible, through observing the behaviour of the float, to identify the species of fish which has caused the movement of the float.

Bites vary according to :

(a) species of fish;
(b) depth of waters at which fishing;
(c) type of bait on the hook, and
(d) the method of angling used.

For example, the bite of the *roach*, especially that of small specimens, is quick – almost jerky. However, a biggish roach tends to take the bait more quietly, and will often cause the float to slide beneath the surface with barely a preliminary movement. As a rule it is this sort of float behaviour, coupled with an immediate strike, which engages the roach. The quick, jerky bite rarely results in a fish being basketed.

The *perch*, on the other hand, causes the float to bob about two, or even three or more times, and then draws it under the surface. The time to strike is when the float disappears.

Pike, in still waters, take leisurely when live-baiting is used. It is necessary to wait until the bobbing float has well and truly disappeared before making a long, firm strike.

Bream give a variety of float signals. This fish has been described as standing on its head to take bait off the bottom, and it is this method of taking which gives the float an unmistakable action. Usually, when a bream takes, the float starts to quiver then rises in the water, falls flat on the surface, then goes under and disappears. The problem is exactly when to strike while all this is going on! Personally, I prefer to wait until the float, having lain flat on the surface, is *beginning* to slide under. A firm strike then usually engages the fish.

The bream can ring the changes on this action: sometimes they will make the float travel about without going under the surface: this may also mean that a small perch has taken the bait, but usually this directional bite indicates a bronze bream.

Tench usually take by showing slight movements on the float, followed by a brief pause, then more float movements followed by a slanting sliding under the surface. The time to strike is when the float starts to slide under.

Carp, when taken with float tackle, usually signal by a sharp dip and cruising off of the float. It is not usual, however, for float tackle to be used by the carp fisherman, the leger and paternoster being methods more generally employed.

Surface Float Fishing. This is a pleasant method. It is also a good method to use when rudd fishing. First of all fish should be attracted into the area by throwing pieces of crust on to the surface. The tackle required is, preferably, a self-cocking float with a light trace from 18 to 24 in.

54

below the float. The hook is baited with breadcrust which should float upon the water surface. If paste or gentle is used the baited hook will sink. Should, therefore, either of these two baits be used a small piece of cork should be placed on the line, about a foot above the hook, and secured with a small shot.

Other Equipment for the Angler. Keep nets pose a controversial problem. For the match fisherman one has to admit that keep nets are essential. But are keep nets essential for the non-competitive angler? Certainly, the size of keep net which is necessary has to be considered very carefully and a walk along most river banks or other waters' edges will show that many keep nets in use are far too small.

Too small a keep net means that fishes crowded into these sort of contraptions become injured. They lose their protective coat of slime, they receive damaged scales when crowded together. Sometimes their fins get damaged against the mesh, and they have been known to get their gills entangled. A small keep net means that when fish retained therein are ultimately returned to the water, a large proportion of them are injured or dying. An injured fish means, in all probability, a doomed fish unable to evade its natural enemies. Too small a keep net is an abomination and a source of much unnecessary cruelty. I am often astonished that anglers who would condemn a fellow angler for catching and retaining a freshwater fish for the table (such as carp, which are popular in certain quarters), although considering themselves true sportsmen actually kill considerably more fish through the use of small keep nets!

Personally, and here I am quite prepared to stick my neck out, I consider that for pleasure angling, as opposed to competition fishing, there is no need to use a keep net at all. I know that some anglers consider that fish caught and immediately released are supposed to spoil one's chances of catching more, but this is surely a reflection on the angler's own skill. I would like to see a complete ban and prohibition on keep nets unless used in a competition, and even then there should be a minimum size limit. Today the manufacturers have at last realized this and have agreed on minimum size limits, a step in the right direction, but still not quite far enough. The minimum size recommended is still far too small.

If a fisherman is prepared to land, measure, weigh, and (perhaps) photograph his fish, then all this should be carried out in as short a time as possible and the fish returned to the water without having to be confined in a cruel mesh prison. This is not sentimentality, but a true appreciation of the facts.

A balance, for the man who keeps accurate records, is necessary and a small spring balance, such as the 'Little Samson', fits easily into the pocket of angling jacket or holdall. This type of spring balance can be obtained in a variety of sizes, weighing by ounces up to 4 lb (in the small size) up to 25 lb by 8 oz in the largest. They cost only a few shillings each.

The float fisherman will find he will need other items of equipment such as stools, angler's umbrella, carry-all, and so on. An uncomfortable angler is, usually, an unsuccessful one. To the general public the spectacle of anglers sitting on stools beneath large umbrellas on a pouring wet day may seem ludicrous. Not so, they are enjoying their sport far more comfortably than the spectator sportsman watching a soccer match, for instance, under similar miserable weather conditions, and who relies upon body heat, generated by thousands of fellow fans, to keep him warm.

Angling conditions vary according to the time of the year. For fishing in the hot summer months the angler can go lightly equipped, though a light mac or raincoat will be regarded as a necessary piece of emergency equipment. For the colder months, and especially winter fishing, the angler will require some warm clothing, preferably with string vest and drawers as underclothing. Too many jerseys or pullovers do not keep one warm, but are apt to impede the circulation and interfere with casting. A waistcoat made of newspaper or brown paper, and worn under the outer coat, serves to keep chilly winds at bay.

I like the modern anorak for winter fishing. The hood can be worn to keep icy winds off the back of one's neck. I do not like the modern tendency to wear a woollen bobble-cap for winter work: the ski-cap, too, is unsuitable. An old trilby or even a sou'-wester is best for wet days as it keeps the rain off the face, and prevents it spilling down one's neck.

Footwear – the angler will have his own fancy. For summer, protection against spiny plants is sufficient: but for winter most anglers will prefer gum-boots and sea-boot stockings.

Though one's hands can become chilled and make it extremely difficult to hold a rod, I prefer no gloves to a thick pair. Trouser pockets make excellent gloves as the body warmth from the legs proves! But mittens have their uses. Again, the angler knows his own resistance to the cold and the choice is his own.

Unless the banks of the water are covered with snow, or frost, the angler should avoid wearing light coloured clothes, and though in summer light garments are desirable, the glaring white shirt should be avoided. This type of clothing acts as a warning to the fishes and scares them away from the angler's vicinity. There are exceptions, however. I have fished the Thames near London, where picnic parties have been on the river bank, with transistor radios blaring away, and the picnickers have been wearing light and gaudy clothing, even white shirts. The fish have come to accept these goings-on at weekends as normal, and an angler can wear a very white shirt, as bright as a TV advertisement, and basket his fish without any trouble.

An excellent item of equipment is the Effgeeco combined seat and pack. An angler can stow all his gear in the pack and use it as a seat. But a lot depends upon how the angler is going to travel to the water. If he travels in a coach with a party of anglers, there is generally plenty of room to store gear, and not too far to carry it to the waterside. The car owner too is in a good position from this angle. The cyclist and the motorcyclist will be concerned, not only with weight, but how to stow the paraphernalia, while the pedestrian will find that he has to compromise with rod, reel, minimum tackle, and a haversack. Fortunately there are many lightweight stools and chairs available today. I use, when travelling as a pedestrian angler, a small stool which folds down to a size $9 \times 6 \times \frac{3}{4}$ in. and yet opens out to a comfortable angling seat and weighs only 24 oz.

A better type of stool is the one with a tubular alloy frame and canvas seat. With a height of about 13 in. and a weight of about 20 oz, it costs just over £1 and can be obtained with a backrest as well for a little more.

Haversacks are a very popular accessory. It is a mistake to buy a cheap haversack, and the ex-w.d. haversacks and respirator cases on the market are really not suitable at all. A good haversack should have a waterproof lining, detachable for cleaning, and be large enough to take most of the angler's tackle, and, perhaps, some fish.

An essential, to protect rods from damage, is a good rod holdall. These should be bought long enough to take the rod and landing nets and can vary from 4 to $5\frac{1}{2}$ ft in length. One word of warning, see that the holdall has a studded leather bottom and that your name and address is boldly printed on it. Every week holdalls are lost, often containing valuable tackle, and, I am afraid it has to be mentioned, some of these losses are not due so much to carelessness on the angler's part, as to light-fingered gentry who are adept at stealing gear while the angler concerned is busy with something else: an indelibly printed name helps to deter such thieves.

In addition to the foregoing items, the angler will find that he will acquire pieces of equipment, from time to time, which, regarded perhaps as 'gimmicks' in the first place, become very important to him as time goes on. Typical of these items are tackle and float wallets, plastic boxes into which hooks, flies, swivels, and so forth can be placed.

These latter become indispensable to the angler when fitted with small compartments, and with clear plastic tops.

A good multi-purpose knife, the kind so beloved by schoolboys, complete with disgorger, shot opener, line cutter, scissors, shot fastener, as well as sharp blade and can-opener, is one item of equipment which the angler soon finds he cannot dispense with. If the knife has a bottle-opener or corkscrew attached then it is a veritable king of angler's knives!

I have left the umbrella until last. Large in diameter like a golf umbrella, the fancy colours of the latter must be dispensed with. Dark green is a good colour and a 36 in. umbrella is the best size. The poles should be strong, certainly not less than 1 in. diameter, and it should be possible to adjust the umbrella to a wide range of positions, otherwise it is most difficult trying to get the necessary tilt on a sloping river bank.

Chapter 4

BOTTOM FISHING

BOTTOM FISHING refers to fishing with the baited hook on the bottom of the river, pond, or other water. As 'laying on' using float tackle has already been discussed as one form of angling it should be understood that the term 'bottom fishing' refers to fishing without the float.

'Legering' and 'paternostering' are the two principal methods of bottom fishing.

When float fishing there is a length of line and/or cast hanging from the surface of the water: when the leger is used the baited hook lies on the bottom, together with two or more feet of cast, and the latter is less likely to be spotted by the fish.

Legering is very effective in fast running rivers, but can also be used in slow moving and still waters. Firstly, let us consider the makeup of a typical leger (Fig. 7). The leger consists of running line, a special portion of the cast on which the leger weight is attached, and the hook. It is sound practice to use a fine wire for the portion of cast upon which the leger weight slides as the movement of the weight will usually fray or weaken gut or monofilament casts. To make up the leger attach the hook-line to about 18 to 24 in. of fine wire. Just above the hook-line attach a small split-shot or piece of lead wire. The purpose of this is to act as a stop and prevent the leger weight from sliding down on to the baited hook. Alternatively, instead of shot or fine wire a small swivel may be used. Now thread the wire through the hole in the bored lead, preferably the bullet type, or the versatile 'Capta' lead by means of its swivel, then attach the wire by means of a loop to the running line.

Angling conditions will decide the size of the leger

weight to be used. It is obvious that the faster the water the heavier the lead. Again, the object of the leger is to allow the fish to take the bait without feeling the weight of the lead. When a fish takes the bait he draws the wire through the bullet : if the leger weight is too heavy the fish may feel its drag and will promptly let the bait go. The bullet must be heavy enough to hold the bottom and allow the fine wire to move about in it, yet not so heavy that it will signal to the fish that all is not well. The leger weight must not be so light that if a biggish fish swims upwards he will lift it off the bottom without drawing the wire through it. Experimentation, experience, commonsense, and compromise will provide the correct answer to the problem – 'what leger weight to use?'

When the baited hook is cast out the angler should then reel in until the line is tight. Now with most forms of angling it is best to keep the rod in hand so that the strike may be made quickly. In legering, however, it is best to lay the rod down, using a special rod rest which may vary from a simple stick with a vee-shaped head to an expensive and complicated cradle.

As there is no float to indicate to the angler when a fish is interested other methods have to be used. A common form is to keep the line tight and watch the rod tip, any trembling of the rod point usually indicating a bite. Or, a method dying out, keep the hand on the rod but have the line over the back of the fingers. This indicates when bites are being made, but, unless bites are very frequent, this method can become tiresome.

Another method is to stick a blob of paste, about the size of a damson, on the running line between reel and bottom ring. When the blob jumps about it is an indication that a bite is being made. A piece of paper, folded over the line, can also be used.

With legering the strike should not be hard. It should be firm and dragging, otherwise the fish will be lost.

Float fishing over large stretches of water can be unsatisfactory as long casts may be necessary, and, without a boat, it might not be possible to get among feeding fish. The leger does enable the angler to make very long casts.

Today it is possible to purchase rods designed specially for legering. This rod does not require to be as long as the match or float rod, and 8 ft is quite a handy length for legering. The leger rod must be more substantial than the match rod, and able to cast fairly heavy weights.

The first thing which the beginner will notice about legering is that, despite the advice given about a quiet approach to the fishing spot, the hints on sober clothing, and as little movement on the waterside as possible, even the slightest conversation being forbidden, the lightest leger weight invariably goes into the water with a terrific splash! This is unavoidable. However, as the weight sinks at once it does not seem to have any adverse effect on the fish.

When legering ground-baiting can be done by making up a paste of bread and the hook bait, be it paste, gentles, or worms. This mixture is squeezed round the leger lead and the cast made. This puts the groundbait in the right spot.

Another useful dodge is to loop a matchstick lightly on to the line below the lead and then squeeze the groundbait round this.

From legering we turn to paternostering. The paternoster is a deadly tackle. I do not think, however, that it is quite as popular as it used to be as many anglers seem to prefer the leger. However, among sea anglers it retains its popularity.

No one can explain how the paternoster got its name. I subscribe, however, to the theory that it derives from the days when the monks and lay brothers used to fish the monastic ponds for the Friday fish and, casting out, would piously repeat, in Latin, the Lord's Prayer – or 'Pater Noster' – 'give us this day our daily bread.' Certainly, it is an ancient method, more certainly it is an effective one, especially when used against pike or perch.

The sketch (Fig. 7) shows how this tackle is made up, and variations of it, but in the main it consists of a trace about 30 in. in length with two or more short traces to which hooks are attached. The lead weight is at the bottom of the trace so that all the hooks are above it.

The individual hook traces should be from 6 to 10 in. in length. Lead to lowest hook-link should be from about 18 to 24 in. according to the nature of the water bottom. If the bottom is very weedy, or very muddy, then distance from lead to hook-link may be three or four feet or even more in order to keep the bait above the weed or prevent it sinking into the soft mud, and disappearing from sight of the fishes.

Paternostering is best done from a boat or jetty as the bait can be gently swung or lowered into the water. When fishing from the bank, a long cast means that the hooks are often too near the bottom, and may even rest in the weeds. When pike fishing it is customary to use a treble hook and the trace as well as the hook-link should be of fine twisted wire. Below the hook-link it is usual to have a monofilament trace to the lead so that in event of a hook-up only the lead is lost.

Instead of using a paternoster rig so that the hooks are clear of the bottom, it may be used somewhat after the manner of the leger in that the tackle is cast out, with the lead lying away from the angler and with the line tight. This probably means that the lower hook is on the bottom and the upper hook clear. As with the leger the rod should be rested and a bite indicator of a bobbin of dough fixed on to the running line.

This type of paternostering is sometimes called 'low' paternostering, and though it is not in common use it is very effective for fishing large lakes or ponds as it allows the angler to get into deep water some distance from the casting point.

When live-baiting with minnow or gudgeon for perch, the paternoster can be lowered into likely holds and when the line is correctly tensioned the live-bait is free to swim about in a natural manner.

For paternoster fishing I prefer to use a centre-pin reel, though there is no reason why a fixed-spool type should not be used. A similar rod to that used for leger fishing is required and, if pike are the quarry, fairly substantially built.

*   *   *

Though I have mentioned some types of leads in dealing with float fishing, the leger enthusiast and the paternoster angler will find special lead weights which have been designed for their methods of fishing. Each type of lead is quite distinct and for a particular use. Some leads are designed for use over gravelly or hard bottoms, others are flattish in shape so that they will not sink into soft mud and help to bury the line. Others are streamlined in shape, to assist in casting by overcoming air resistance, and, of greater importance, to allow moving currents to flow easily over and round them.

Though sea anglers, as will be seen in a later chapter, have special leads for their sport, none the less they may use freshwater style leads, though usually in a much heavier weight range.

The following notes on lead types should help the angler in his leger and paternostering forays in fresh water.

'Capta' leads (Fig. 6). These are a proprietary lead and quite unusual in design. I shall not forget my first reaction when I was called upon to test a batch of these leads when they appeared on the market. 'Another gimmick,' I thought. 'Something else to assist in extracting money from the angler's so-called bottomless purse.' I was quite wrong.

The original 'Capta' leads were produced with the freshwater angler in mind, varying from $\frac{1}{8}$ oz up to 1 oz, and were available singly or in attractive plastic boxes containing an assortment of that weight range. The leads are unique. They are pyramidal in shape with a brass swivel built into their top. Their flat base enables them to lie on the bed of the river, or pond, or sea, and the water pressure exerted from above keeps them in position, while their shape permits currents to ride past them without moving them. This proves of great value when fishing over muddy or soft bottoms as the wide spread of this lead counteracts the tendency of the lead to sink into the ooze. I found that when retrieving the lead the shape gave it a lifting or kite action yet at the same time allowed the angler to keep it low in the water until the last few feet of line were recovered. The built-in-swivel, of course, gives the lead good anti-kink qualities.

This is a good all-round lead useful for spinning, legering, and even float fishing. A great advantage which this lead has over more conventional types is the fact that only half the normal weight may be used! If one normally uses, say, a $\frac{1}{2}$ oz bullet, then a $\frac{1}{4}$ oz 'Capta' is quite sufficient.

The 'Capta' does not, owing to its poor aerodynamical shape, cast as easily as the 'Arlesey' bomb, and is at a slight disadvantage with the latter when used under very windy conditions : but it scores better along the line otherwise.

Arlesey bombs (Fig. 6). These are streamlined leads with a swivel built into their tails. They are available in weights from $\frac{1}{4}$ oz upwards to $1\frac{1}{2}$ oz and may be used for spinning, legering, and float legering. Owing to their shape, which reduces air resistance, they cast better than flat or coffin leads.

Flat leger. These are really flat leads with a hole drilled lengthwise : call them flat tubes if you like. They are used for leger work with split shot as described earlier and can be used in muddy or soft bottoms where a bullet lead would sink.

Paternoster. These are small pear-shaped or tear-drop-shaped leads with a swivel or link attachment built into the tail. The Arlesey bomb is really a refinement of this lead. They may be used for leger and spinning as well as paternoster work.

Spiral. A long lead with a spiral groove running its length. Used for spinning work and easily attachable and detachable.

Chapter 5

SPINNING FOR COARSE FISH

SPINNING IS an exciting method of fishing. Not all anglers are the contemplative folk who like to sit or lie and wait for float to dip, tip to swing, or bobbin of dough to dance. Their temperament is of a more active nature. They are hunters. They like to seek out their quarry and, in place of trap or ambush by cunningly concealed hook-impregnated food, try to tempt the fish itself into hunting.

When seeking the predators, pike and perch, anglers will find themselves entered into a controversy as to which is the best method – to spin or to live-bait. In my own experience, as in that of many other anglers, spinning seems to account for more fish than live-baiting, whereas live-baiting seems to account for the bigger specimens.

But, to me, the main attraction in spinning lies not in the fact that it accounts for the fighting predators, and that it is more active than float or bottom fishing, but from the fact that spinning is more productive in the winter months. Because one is moving about and casting continually, even on the coldest of days, the angler will keep himself reasonably warm : the angler who legers a deep hole under wintry conditions will have to keep himself well wrapped up and, being static, will in any event still be half-frozen.

Tackle

Compared with bottom fishing and float tackle the spinning outfit is much more expensive. Not that the rods are more expensive, but the outlay comes in the purchase of lures. Pike and perch lures can cost anything from 1s. 6d. each to 15s. or more. And if the angler should lose a couple of these in one day, as can easily happen, it does tend to make the outing expensive. The high cost of spinning lures, coupled with the high loss rate, has probably induced many anglers to exploration of do-it-yourself lure manufacturing, and thereafter to home building of other items of angling equipment.

Compared with a bottom rod a spinning rod is much shorter. It will probably be from 4 to 6 ft in length. Though it is stiff enough to cast a bait of over 1 oz in weight, it has to be whippy throughout its length to the butt. However, the spinning rod must be well chosen with regard to the conditions under which it will be used.

A river or reservoir with a high bank will need a longer rod than one with a low bank, otherwise retrieving the lure after each cast does become difficult. Today most spinning rods are built of glass-fibre and designs from Norway and

8 A multiplier reel

the United States are becoming very popular. Rods from both these countries are built lightly, yet strongly.

Spinning and bait-casting rods are becoming popular with young anglers. This is due, I think, to the lightness and simplicity of the tackle as spinning outfits consist of (usually) a light rod with a fixed-spool reel, or an equally light rod in combination with what is termed a multiplier reel (Fig. 8).

The multiplier is very popular overseas and a great favourite with sea-anglers here. It is better than the fixed-spool reel for distance casting, and for use with heavy baits or weights.

The multiplier derives its name from the fact that the drum, through a system of gears, revolves at a greater speed than the recovery handle. It is also equipped with an even winding device which ensures that the recovered line is laid evenly over the drum surface. Incidentally, unlike the conventional reel (whether centre-pin or fixed spool), the multiplier, in common with the closed-face reel, is designed for use on top of the rod for both casting and recovery.

The great disadvantage of the multiplier is the time taken to learn to use it properly. Until the art of casting has been mastered the angler will make bigger and better birds' nests and tangles than he had hitherto thought possible! But the centre-pin technique is useful here for the multiplier can be mastered by braking with the finger in centre-pin style on the reel rim. When recovering a line whether for recasting or bringing a fish in, the return is rapid, and if much casting is done, this takes a certain amount of hard work out of the game. This is important because though the complete outfit may be light and the rod short, none the less correct working of the outfit means plenty of work. Light tackle must be worked hard.

Though the normal spinning rod follows the general pattern of cork handle into which the rod is fastened, whether one or two-piece, there is another type of rod on the market which uses a short off-set handle (Fig. 3). These are generally built with a light metal collet or chuck into which a short top is fitted and many anglers use a rod top with this gadget as a short spinning rod. For multiplier reels, and for closed-face reels, the offset handle rod is a good proposition and I use such a combination for both fresh- and salt-water angling.

Of fixed-spool reels the Intrepid (British) and the Mitchell (French) are probably the best known, and of centre-pin reels the Strikeright and those made by Young (both British concerns) enjoy great popularity. For multiplier reels for freshwater spinning one must look overseas, to Canada, to the United States, and to Norway and Sweden. For easy long casting from finely built free running spools the Swedish ABU models are unapproachable. However, the Alvey (Australian) sidecaster is an excellent proposition for the angler who prefers his outfit to be as simple as possible. After all, the simpler apparatus is the less likely it is to go wrong, and should that happen there are less matters to put right.

The closed-face reel is comparatively new on the British scene. Those imported from United States and from Sweden have been well tested in their home conditions, and though some angling writers have referred to them as looking like bicycle-bells, none the less they are a sound practical job. I use a closed-face reel for sea spinning and can vouch for its efficiency.

The closed-face reel differs from conventional reels in that the drum is covered. Built like a fixed-spool reel, to which family it belongs, in place of a pickup arm the closed face is utilized. The line is threaded through the centre of the closed face or cone. At the base of the reel is a thumb-operated control lever. When the control lever is pressed down it automatically retracts a pickup pin and the line becomes free to run from the spool and at the same time traps the line until the thumb lever is released. Full details of the closed-face reel are given in the chapter on casting.

Lures

Spinning for freshwater fish, apart from game fish, is usually restricted to pike and perch, though on the Continent large roach are often taken on special spoon spinning baits. Though spinning can be done with a dead natural bait using special flights or mounts, the artificial bait is more popular.

The novice is strongly advised to keep his spinning tackle as simple as possible.

Though lures festooned with hooks seem an attractive proposition, a moment's reflection will show that this is not really so. The more hooks on a lure, the greater the chances are of that lure getting entangled in weeds or other underwater obstructions. As most entanglements mean the loss of fairly expensive lures, it is better to cut down on the number of hooks and, in practice, a lure with but a single hook, double or treble, is without doubt the best proposition.

In any case, if the hook is at the rear of the lure this is the part most likely to be contacted by the fish, and other hooks are not so well placed. Too many hooks on a lure also pose the problem of handling when a fish is landed. To get one hook out is one thing, but to manage three or more trebles in safety is something else.

Lures may be categorized as follows :

Spoons, wobblers, artificial minnows (or other fish), plugs, dazzlers, all of which may be floating or non-floating.

The spoon is what it sounds like – a spoon. This may

9 'Kidney' spoon bait

vary in size from a tea-spoon up to two or more inches. They also vary in shape. The 'Colorado' has a couple of vanes at the head, a leaded bar through the long axis, and has a treble hook mounted at the rear on to which a tuft of red wool is attached. The spoon is usually painted red inside and the outside left shiny.

The 'Kidney' is shaped like that organ. It is only attached at the top and is not dressed with wool or tinsel (Fig. 9).

The 'Devon' or artificial minnow (Fig. 10) is a small torpedo type of lure, gold, silver, or blue in colour. It has a pair of vanes at the head which cause it to revolve round the wire mount when drawn through the water. As in the case of the 'Colorado' the hook, a treble, is mounted well to the rear of the minnow body.

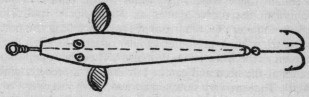

10 Typical 'Devon' minnow

A plug bait may consist of wood or transparent plastic and is usually built to represent a small fish. Equipped with a sloping nose, or with a vane, it is generally a floating lure which dives and wobbles when drawn through the water.

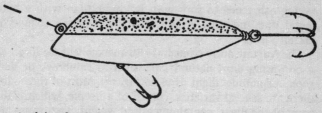

11 A plain plug bait

12 Jointed, diving, vaned plug bait

Types of this lure may be single body, or jointed, and the action of all plugs is to represent a frightened, wounded, or sickly fish (Figs. 11 and 12).

From simple wooden lures with a shaped head causing it

71

to dive and wobble, the plug may be manufactured in transparent plastic. Typical examples are the famous 'Heddon' range which, in various forms, rejoice in such American descriptive names as 'Super Sonic' and 'Tiny Crazy Crawler'. Of plugs suited for pike fishing the best I have tried have been the tubular plastic Swedish lures known as the ABU 'Hi-Lo Wobblers'. These have adjustable vanes at the head and can be retrieved at a predetermined depth. They are very slow sinkers and weigh just over $\frac{1}{2}$ oz.

A very popular lure for pike and perch is the wagtail. This has a body made of rubber or plastic material and is given a fishlike colour and appearance. In line with the 'Colorado' and 'Devon' it has a couple of propeller vanes or blades at the head, but has two treble hooks attached. The tails of the 'fish' overlap and are free to flap and wave in an intriguing manner. As the body of the lure is soft, the taking fish tends to stay with it longer than with a hard metal one and thus gives the angler a better chance of taking a fish.

The wagtail, aptly named, is also an excellent sea lure.

For using dead natural bait, such as minnows or gudgeon, a spinning 'flight' is used (Fig. 13). Most of these, and there are several varieties, consist of a needle, which is the body of the flight, containing a lead weight. Two vanes are attached to the head and two small treble hooks trail from the head on fine wire. Dead natural bait is attached to the flight by pushing on to the needle as far as it will go. Then, with either an elastic rubber hand, or fine wire, the two trebles are lashed to the side of the dead bait, whereupon the lure is ready for action.

To prevent the line kinking and twisting an anti-kink device must be used. This generally consists of a lead weight attached to the trace above the swivels and so shaped that its mass lies below the line. Alternatively a vane, or half-moon, of celluloid or lead may similarly be attached. The principle is that of a ship's keel, using the water pressure against its surface to prevent the line rotating and thereby twisting and kinking.

Between bait and line there should be a wire spinning trace. This should have a swivel at each end and should be about two feet in length. Combined with anti-kink device, the use of the three swivels (two on the trace and one in the lure) should eliminate all chances of twist in the line.

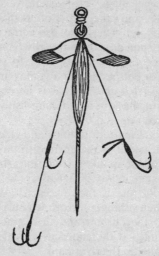

13 Spinning flight on to which a natural dead fish is mounted

The Technique of Spinning

Spinning is an artistic method of taking coarse fish : it has the additional advantage that it is a clean method of fishing. By clean I mean that it is not necessary to collect a lot of bait such as gentles, grubs, worms, bread, cheese, or other substances. Spinning tackle also takes up a lot less room than float or leger tackle. For one thing there is no need for bags of groundbait, there is no need for a chair or stool for the angler to sit upon and a whole selection of lures will fit into a small box carried in the angler's pocket.

Spinning consists of presenting a lure to a fish or fishes in such a manner that it appears as a tempting morsel and

73

induces the quarry to take it. From the dressing of some lures it may also be that the presentation of the lure is to arouse ferocity or the equivalent of anger in one's quarry, causing it to attack the bait.

Lures may be spun at all depths. Heavy lures, such as Devons and some plugs, are generally spun near the bottom. Wagtails, and other types of spoon and plug, may be spun in mid-water. There are also surface lures, chiefly plugs, which are spun near to or actually on the surface.

When spinning there is rarely need to strike as in the manner of float or bottom fishing, the movement of the lure usually does the trick and all that is necessary to get the hooks firmly into the jaw of a taking fish is a slightly increased pressure on the rod.

Spinning is not a matter of chuck and chance. The water temperature, the speed of the current (if any) and the time of the year all affect spinning conditions. In cold weather the fish lie deeper and it is necessary to fish the lower waters. A heavier lure is then necessary, or some weight added to it. When fishing a stream it is usual to make the first cast across the current and then gradually vary the angle of casts until, at the end, one is casting downstream and almost parallel to the river bank.

There are two methods of recovery of lure. Firstly, there is the straightforward wind in after the lure has reached the correct depth. The lure is retrieved at a constant speed. Secondly, a little line is recovered at a time. Thus the angler may make four or five turns of the reel handle, and then slow down for a couple of turns, and then give four or five more quick turns, and so on. This imitates the movement of a startled fish and is more natural than continuous smooth recovery. Alternatively, and the method I like best, the lure is recovered at varying speeds and the rod tip is raised and lowered between times so that the fish not only appears to dart, but also wobbles and tumbles about in the manner of a sick or wounded creature.

It is necessary to keep winding in the lure until the very last moment and a bait is often taken just when the angler is ready to lift the lure from the water. This is so where one is casting over shallow water into deep water, for a frightened minnow or immature fish will naturally make for the shallows when pursued by a predator, and it is in the shallows where the bite is finally made.

From time to time it is also advisable to change the lure to an identical pattern but with an opposite direction of rotation. This is to take out any twist which might have been put into the line in spite of anti-kink devices.

Pike fishing can be successful if a dead bait is used on a wobbler flight. This is better than an artificial lure in many instances because it can be worked slowly, something which a heavy bait renders impossible, and once a pike has attacked it it is not likely to let it go as occasionally happens when plastic, wood, or metal lures or spinners are being used.

Casting

Casting with the different types of reels must be thoroughly mastered by the spinning enthusiast. Casting with the fixed-spool reel or threadline reel as it was once termed is a simple enough matter and it is important that the beginner learns to cast not only to a given distance, but with accuracy to a given mark.

To cast with a fixed-spool reel, hold the rod handle with the leg or foot of the reel between second and third fingers. The line should be trapped against the rod handle with the forefinger. The pickup is then dropped so that it is retracted and leaves the line free for casting. At this stage only the pressure of your forefinger against the line, pressing it against the rod handle, prevents it spilling off the reel. You are now ready to cast.

Look at the spot where you intend the bait to be placed and point the rod directly towards it, then bring the rod back in a sharp sweep to the 12 o'clock position. This should be done by using the wrist only. Now, without pausing bring the rod forward again with pressure of wrist and thumb and when the rod reaches the 10 o'clock position

75

release the line by lifting the forefinger. The line will peel off and the lure should fly straight towards the selected point.

If the cast has been too powerful, or you wish to stop the lure before it hits the water, just trap the line against the handle again with the forefinger.

If you have been careful the lure will have flown correctly. However, what often happens is that the lure either flies almost straight up, or hits the water almost at your own feet! The first is due to the fact that the line has been released too soon : the other is due to the fact that the line has been held trapped too long.

As soon as the bait hits the water and the slack line has been reeled in, the rod tip should be lowered to a horizontal position.

I think at this stage I should explain about the clutch in a thread-line or fixed-spool reel. Because a light line is being used the reel contains a slipping clutch, which, when properly adjusted, slows up the run of a fish without breaking the line. Furthermore, the drag or clutch can be set at any time during the playing of a fish, and as a matter of practice the tension of the clutch should be checked before making a cast. One soon gets accustomed to doing this and it is done quite simply by pulling the line with the free hand while preventing the reel handle from turning.

Whatever the temptation there is one rule which must not be broken when fishing with the fixed-spool reel : as the sole function of the clutch is to allow a strong fish to draw line without causing a breakage or tangle the angler MUST NEVER WIND IN AGAINST THE SLIPPING CLUTCH WHEN FIGHTING A FISH. If he does so the line will kink terribly.

Casting with the multiplier, or bait casting as it is termed in America, is a different matter. First of all the angler must realize that whereas the forefinger has been used to hold the line in the case of casting with a fixed-spool reel, it is his thumb which now assumes importance. In fact, correct thumb control is the key to good multiplier casting.

The rod is used as hitherto described. First of all it is

pointed at the target and then with the thumb of the casting hand resting on the reel and pressing slightly against the line and spool flange, the rod is raised to a 2 o'clock position.

The rod tip is then lowered slightly by dropping the hand, remember it is the wrist which performs all the casting, then the wrist is flicked upwards and the forearm slightly raised so that the rod tip is lifted to a 12 o'clock position. Then quickly, smartly, the rod is checked and the wrist is snapped forwards and downwards. As the rod point reaches the 1 o'clock position the thumb pressure on the line is reduced sufficiently to allow the bait to shoot forwards. The rod continues dropping until a position about 3 o'clock is reached. The flight of the lure towards the target must be watched and thumb pressure must be applied to slow its speed down. As it reaches the target the spool is stopped by thumb pressure so that the lure will drop correctly.

It is absolutely essential that the backward and forward motion of the rod must be done in one movement, without pause.

Spinning, using a centre-pin reel, is quite a simple matter. To cast the lure, line is first stripped off the reel by the left hand, assuming that the rod is held in the right hand, of a sufficient length to allow the bait to be cast into the target area. The stripped line is allowed to fall into loose coils at the feet of the angler. It is sometimes advantageous to lay a piece of plastic material, or a handkerchief upon the ground, so that the loose coils of line will not be caught up by grass or weeds, causing a snag.

When ready to cast, about 5 ft of line should swing from the rod tip so that the bait has a pendulum motion. The caster should then half-face the spot into which he is going to cast the lure and hold the line in his left hand. The bait is then put into a pendulum motion after which the rod tip is swung into the direction of the target and at the same time the loose line is released by the left hand. The bait should then fly out to the desired spot.

The angler then waits for a moment or so, according to

depth of water, speed of current, and so forth, to allow the lure to sink and then, lowering the rod point to within about a foot of the surface, begins to recover the line, not by turning the reel, but by drawing it in with the left hand and at the same time drawing the rod tip back with his right.

It is possible to cast from a free-running centre-pin reel, and this is done in a similar manner to using a multiplier, except that the tip of the forefinger is used as a brake or check against the rim of the spool instead of the thumb. When casting in this style, also called the Nottingham style, recovery is made by winding in on the reel. The correct technique is to wind slowly for a few yards, then drag the bait through the water a yard or so by swinging the rod tip, stop winding for a moment, then commence winding again, and repeat until the lure has been recovered.

Whatever the style or tackle used, there is one important rule to remember: in fast waters the lure must be recovered at a slower rate than on slow or still waters, otherwise it will be brought to the surface and kept there.

For many years I have made it a point to practise casting over dry land before visiting a fishing point. I remember on one occasion, practising in a field over which I normally shoot, at 6.30 one summer's morning, I found a policeman watching me over a hedge. He obviously thought that I was barmy, fishing over dry land. However, I explained to him what I was doing and even induced him to have a go!

By practising over dry land, with a lure or its equivalent weight and *no* hook on the line, and given plenty of wide open space, the angler can practise simple casting, and then develop casting underhand, sideways and from a backwards position. Nowadays one reads in angling papers that one should be able to cast over a hundred yards with modern equipment. This leads to a lot of wrong thinking. It is nice to know that with modern equipment one is able to achieve enormous distances, with accuracy, but the trend towards long-distance casting is wrong. It stands to sense that whereas you may cast across a wide river to fish within a foot of the opposite bank, the angler on the other side can be doing the same! Both of you are then being discourteous to each other, and furthermore it shows that one would be just as successful in dropping the lure along one's own bank!

I think that too many anglers today, from what I have seen at the waterside, cast over and beyond their fish. That is also one reason why fish seem to take the lure at the end of the spin, just before it is lifted from the water.

When playing a fish on the lure there is a common error made by keeping the rod too near the vertical. The injunction 'keep your rod tip up' is all right, to a point, but 'up' should not be at an angle of more than 50° to 60°, otherwise all the strain of the struggle will be thrown against the top and middle joints and a damaged rod may well result. When recovering the line by dropping the rod tip the rod should only be dropped to about 30°, otherwise too much strain will be thrown on the line itself and the reel, and the action of the rod will be wasted.

Again, no matter what outfit one is using, though the fish should be held and kept on the move, he must not be held hard, otherwise, especially in the case of a fixed-spool outfit, the fish will be lost.

A fish, except a very small specimen, should not be lifted from the water and wound in to hand. The function of a rod and reel is to cast a line and recover it, and it is not designed to substitute for a crane or for weight lifting. This is especially so in the case of a fixed-spool reel. Large or heavy fish should be brought to the basket through gaffing or netting and instructions on this are given later.

Chapter 6

FLY FISHING FOR COARSE FISH

UNTIL COMPARATIVELY recent years fly fishing was regarded solely as a branch of game fishing, occasionally pursued by a few eccentrics among the coarse fishermen and sometimes by the sea angler. Today the fact that coarse fish may be taken by the fly is accepted and this skilful and artistic method of fishing is finding more converts.

Of coarse fish which give good sport on the fly, dace, rudd, and chub are the most accommodating, but perch may also be taken. One does hear of pike being taken on the fly but though I have tried to find anglers fly fishing specifically for pike I have not found one – this seems to be in the same category as spinning for roach. I admit that, on the Continent, large roach are fished for with a spinner, but the roach which accepts a spinning bait in these islands is a rare fish indeed. Taken on the fly the chub is really worth while; unlike the chub which takes the conventional bait and gives a promising first run followed by a tame submission, the chub which takes the fly gives a continual battle until landed.

Whereas 'dapping' the live insect has sometimes been classed as a special form of angling, it should really be included under the heading of fly fishing. Certainly in this book I shall combine the two together.

There are two different methods of fly fishing, dry and wet fly. In dry fly fishing the angler fishes with fly which floats on the surface of the water, and in the case of the dry fly this is used against a particular fish which the angler has observed feeding. The fly used, in this instance, is as close an imitation as possible to the real thing on which the fish is feeding.

Wet fly fishing is usually divided into two different categories, upstream and downstream fishing. As the title 'wet fly' implies, the lure is submerged below the water surface, and though the angler tries, wherever possible, to cast to a 'rising' fish, he also uses the lure to explore the places where fish are likely to be.

Flies are artificial lures consisting of a hook dressed with materials, such as fur, silk, feathers, to represent a natural insect and, furthermore, there is a slight complication in that the flies may also be tied or dressed to represent one of three stages in the life of the *Ephemeridae* or upright winged flies. These stages are firstly, the larva or nymph stage, secondly the sub-imago or intermediate stage when the flies have hatched out and known to the angler as 'Duns', and finally the stage when the insects are fully matured and have shed their final casings. This last stage is known as the imago stage and in this condition they are known to the fly fisherman as 'Spinners'. In the North of England the Dun stage is also called the 'Bloa'.

In addition to the *Ephemeridae*, the fly fisherman will find that there are other families of insects which are imitated by the fly tyer. These include the *Trichoptera*, or Caddis Flies, and their chief characteristic is that the wings fold back along the body at a slight angle. From this family come the fisherman's 'Sedge' flies, and the 'Alders'. A third family of flies important to the angler is that of the *Perlidae*, and this includes the Stone fly. In these insects the wings cross or overlap the body and lie flat. Other anglers' flies are the *Diptera*, similar to the ordinary house fly, and of course there are various lures tied to represent beetles, craneflies, ants, and moths.

Though this may appear somewhat technical and perhaps a little overfacing to the beginner, it is essential that he gets to know the different flies and, of course, the names by which they are known such as 'March Brown', 'Greenwell's Glory', 'Blue Upright', or 'Coachman'. By purchasing one or two flies, on the advice of the local tackle dealer, the beginner will soon become used to the names and appearance of the patterns.

In addition, of course, to identifying the fly, he must also know when certain species are likely to appear on the water and when they should be used. I have, therefore, included a small table in the chapter dealing with fly fishing for trout, and reference should be made to it by the coarse fish fly angler.

Unfortunately, the idea is rather widely held that fly fishing is for experts only, that it is difficult to master. This is not so. Many novices fail, in the first instance, because they have probably failed to realize that the first essential in fly fishing is to know where the fish is or likely to be, and then try to induce that fish to take the lure. Not only does the dry fly fisherman cast to a particular fish, he must also know where takeable fish are most likely to be in a particular water.

Fly fishing demands the use of a special outfit. The rod must be fairly whippy for wet fly fishing: rather stiff for dry fly fishing. The reel is centre-pin type. A special line must be used and this must be of sufficient size, or weight, to match correctly the action and strength which have been built into the rod.

The best fly lines have a double taper. That is, they taper from a heavy centre-section to short lengths of smaller diameter at each end. This type of line supplies the weight which enables the angler to cast the correct distance with only a light fly on the end. Formerly only oil-dressed silk lines were used for fly fishing, but the modern braided man-made fibre line has proved more reliable. There are usually two types of fly line on the market: one is the solid dressed line, and the other is the hollow floating line, usually known as the bubble line. Personally, I prefer the solid dressed line: it stands up better to wear and tear and is narrower in diameter than the line with the built-in air buoyancy chambers! The hollow lines, I have found, often wear out fairly quickly, and I have been very disappointed with those I have tried.

The fly line is usually about 30 yards long. The coarse fisherman may be surprised to learn this, as he is accustomed to longer sizes on his drum, but the average fly fisherman only casts from 5 to 15 yds! It is because of the shorter casting, coupled with extreme accuracy, that many anglers are discarding the double taper fly line and taking a line with a forward taper only. But the practical angler may prefer the double taper because he can reverse the line between outings, thereby doubling its life! Fly fishing lines are not cheap – a good line will leave one with no change out of £5.

The novice should beware of purchasing too light a line : here the expert opinion of an angling friend or tackle dealer should be sought. *Do not forget that the correct weight of the line is that which matches the rod.*

In the absence of specific information about the water to be fished which determines the length of rod, a good compromise length for a fly rod is between 8 and 9 ft. There are varied opinions about the merits of fibre-glass against built cane. Though I prefer the modern glass rod, there are others who prefer the built cane article and this is largely a matter of personal choice. The older angler will prefer the materials to which he has been accustomed : the newcomer will have no prejudices, though he may lack experience. I would advise, however, that for a first fly rod, the beginner does not commit himself too heavily financially. Later on, when he has mastered the casting and has formed an opinion on the type of rod he requires, he can go ahead and purchase another rod. This time his choice will be based on experience.

The reel must balance the rod. It must have a fairly large drum so that recovery of the line may be quick. It must be uncomplicated in construction in order that it may be easily taken apart for maintenance and oiling. The reel should be large enough to take the correct line plus a backing line of from 25 to 70 yd. The reel diameter may vary from 3 in. (the smallest) to 4 in.

The first difference the beginner will note between the coarse fishing rod he has been used to and the fly rod, is the position of the reel. In the fly rod this is at the end of the butt (except in the case of a double handed fly rod used for salmon fishing and some sea angling), and therefore below the hand of the angler. This has a considerable effect on the feel of a rod when the reel is not fitted to it : and it is only when the reel is fitted to the rod that the angler can select the correct outfit. All must balance, and therefore when purchasing a new rod or reel, the other half of the outfit must be taken along to the tackle shop at the same time and the new selection handled with the appropriate tackle added. It is foolish to purchase either rod or reel separately.

In addition to rod, reel, and line, the angler will require some casts. These are usually about 9 ft in length and tapered at the end to which the fly is tied. For the wet fly fisherman, who may use two or three flies (the extra flies known as 'droppers'), the casts may be bought with dropper casts already tied to the main cast. Casts cost in the region of 1s. each.

So much for the equipment – other items will be required, such as boxes to carry the flies in, a waterproof dressing to make the dry flies float, and so forth, but the angler will already be in possession of most of this.

With regard to the technique of fly fishing, casting, and methods, the reader is referred to the chapter on fly fishing for trout.

Fly fishing

The dace rises freely to the artificial fly of which the best pattern to use, I have found, is a wet fly, 'The Black Gnat'. Some anglers recommend that a gentle also be used with the fly, but personally I feel that this is unnecessary. Gentles alone, even small red worms, may be fished in wet fly fashion, and the addition of an artificial fly is superfluous.

The chub always seems to lie in difficult spots for the fly fisherman! It entails a lot of dry-land practice to be able to cast a fly to a chub who is generally located under boughs overhanging the water. But, good consolation for the fisherman, when the chub takes a fly he is very definite about it and the hook is rarely pulled from his jaws. There is a special type of fly on the market known as a 'Chub' fly. This is a very successful pattern and should be obtained in two or three sizes: the smaller size being used during the daytime and the larger after dusk or on a very dull day. No droppers should be used when chub fishing. Other flies which the chub will take readily are Black Palmer, Red Palmer, and flies tied to represent moths.

The rudd, too, is partial to the artificial fly. He will take similar flies to those fancied by the dace, but sometimes will also take bread paste on a hook fished wet-fly fashion, when he will look at nothing else. When rudd are in taking mood they give excellent sport and I recall one evening on the ponds at Hampstead Heath taking a large basket of rudd on a small Coch-y-Bondhu. Indeed I was so successful that one bottom fisher at the far end of the pond accused me of being a 'Pied Piper' of the angling world!

I have had luck, occasionally, with a roach when fishing for rudd with the fly: but I have never fished for them specifically this way. The best time for fly with the rudd is in the evening during the late summer.

Dace, of course, liking a moving stream, may be fished upstream or down and give the fly fisherman excellent practice in both methods.

Dapping

This means using the natural insect with the fly rod. There are usually two methods. One is to use a boat, letting the rod stand upright with the breeze letting the line stream out ahead, and then gently lowering the rod tip until the bait alights on the water. This is a very popular Irish method of fishing for big lake trout. The other method involves stalking the fish and, from a concealed spot on the bank, gently lowering the bait until it rests on the surface of the water. This is a good method to use for chub. The most popular baits to use are the 'Daddy Long Legs' and the natural Grasshopper.

For chub fishing the best days are those very bright days

with plenty of sun and not too much wind. This ensures that this shyest of fishes is near the surface of the water. Dapping for chub is best carried out after dusk.

I remember that for many seasons I had kept on stressing to a friend that I preferred to catch my coarse fish on the fly. Ultimately he asked me to come along and talk to an angling club on this subject. I did so and was received quite well. However, I received my greatest pleasure when one day an angler who had been a sceptic at that meeting and really tried to ask me a lot of awkward questions, rang me up and said that he had tried out fly fishing on chub. 'I got a beauty,' he yelled into the phone, nearly disrupting my eardrums. 'Couldn't have got him by any other method. Fly fishing for me next time.' It was so. He became a real convert to the art and found that chub, in particular, will respond to the fly when other methods fail.

Chapter 7

COMPETITIONS

THOUGH ANGLING is pursued by an uncounted number of anglers, the casual observer may think that the be all and end all of the coarse fisherman is 'match' or 'competition' fishing. I think that this is because competition fishing takes place at the weekend and therefore the sight of anglers lining the banks of a river or canal becomes more obvious. But, though match fishing may be the only reason for many anglers' ownership of fishing tackle, it does not form the main reason for angling as a whole.

In industrial districts, and within a reasonable travelling distance of such places, match fishing is often the only way in which an angler may fish. There is a shortage of angling waters – indeed, one might say there are too many anglers. Match fishing solves this problem to a great extent. It must be obvious that fish congregate in certain places during certain conditions, and if all anglers arriving for a day's fishing were to try and fish at the same spot chaos would ensue. Now match fishing means that anglers draw for their angling places, and the rest depends upon (a) what fish are available and (b) the angler's skill in making the most of his chances.

Let me state that I am no match fisherman. I take part in other competitions, and have taken part in many sports, but for myself I prefer angling to be a personal, quiet sport and I do not like the betting element which enters into it. But for others it is a choice of match angling or no angling.

The match angler becomes very skilful. He knows how to calculate a swim, what bait to use, and how to use it correctly, and how to hook and keep his fish. He may find that he has to hunt, within the limits of his stretch of water, two or three big fish : again, he may, like one angler in a national contest, have to go all out and land as many small fish as possible, and in this instance the angler landed 400 bleak!

Angling contests may be at club or national level and though the rules for the different competitions may vary slightly, they are intended that each individual angler shall have every chance to show his skill either as an individual or as a member of a team representing club, association, or even country.

The rules are generally the same: an angler is not allowed to disturb the water until the competition starts. This means that he cannot plumb the depth or start to throw in the groundbait until the 'off' signal is given.

Only one rod, line, and hook is allowed to be used at once.

Fish taken must be retained in a keep net until they have been weighed at the end of the contest, after which they must be returned to the water.

Most competitions are arranged on a straightforward angling basis, but there are handicap competitions occasionally in which a good angler has to give away certain weight to less skilful competitors. Some clubs organize competitions for charities, in which the whole of the fees are donated to some good cause or another. Perhaps the angling club will have a prize for the heaviest fish taken on a certain day, or during the season: for the biggest basket made: for the best lady member: for the best junior angler: and even, let it be said, a wooden spoon for the angler with the least weight of fish in a season! There are also competitions in which anglers travel abroad to fish against other associations, or other national teams.

The angler draws a numbered peg at the point where he is to fish and he is limited, therefore, to the water into which he can send his tackle. Once an angler accepts the peg he cannot give up angling if he is not catching fish; he must see the competition period through: otherwise it is like a footballer quitting his team before a match ends.

The National Federation of Anglers has been organizing

annual English Angling Championships since 1906, when seven teams entered, and this has grown so popular that today upwards of 100 teams are represented in this contest.

The Individual (NFA) Championship has been held, also, since 1906, apart from the two World War years.

I have only one criticism to make of match fishing. I have travelled round the country a lot and often, after a match has been fished, seen large numbers of dead or injured fishes floating on the water. Now let me be fair, some of these dead fishes are due to careless anglers who are not fishing in matches, some are due to hooks which have been too far down the fish's throat for disgorging, others have been damaged through too small keep nets. Again pleasure anglers also use too small a keep net.

The object of match fishing is to test the angler's skill: as the fish are to be returned to the water if undersize and returned alive after the weigh-in, *barbless* hooks should in my opinion be used. I know that many anglers disagree with this, pointing out that it is the barb which enables them to bring the fish in.

Many things, controversial measures, have to be introduced into field sports to make sure that there is no unnecessary cruelty. I know that fishes are in the lower orders of life and do not feel pain as we do, but that is not the argument. I advocate the *barbless* hook, not on the grounds of painless hooking, but so that the fish is more likely to be returned undamaged. Again a skilful angler can bring in a fish on a barbless hook and if these were introduced it would be up to the average angler to improve his skill. Barbed hooks for fish for the table, by all means: but where fish are not for retention, then let's be progressive and dispense with the barb.

The skilful man, who hooks and brings his fish in quickly and without fuss, will find no objection to barbless hooks: he does not need the barb to help him, anyway. This is my personal opinion on a controversial subject but I am putting it into print so that the *thinking* angler can consider the implications carefully.

Irrespective of whether competition fishing or just angling for pleasure, there are certain size limits below which fish must be returned to the water alive, except where taken for use as bait. The permitted sizes vary from water to water and as a rule the River Authority licence sets out the permitted sizes.

It is in connection with size that most angling jokes arise. The one that got away is invariably a specimen or record breaker. But, until a fish is landed and weighed, one cannot estimate its weight. There are certain standards which give the approximate weight of a healthy fish in connection with its length: and the angler should study these. For example, a 9 in. perch should weigh about 12 oz : a 12 in. specimen 1 lb. An 8 in. roach should weigh about 4½ oz, but it would have to be about 11 in. to weigh 1 lb. But I think that it is the record fish which attracts a lot of attention, and though few anglers deliberately fish for a record, there can be few prouder men than the angler who takes a fish which becomes, nationally, the biggest landed by fair means by rod and line.

Record Fish

From time to time fish are landed which come to be termed as 'record specimens'. This does not necessarily mean that the particular fish is the largest ever caught: what it does mean is that it is the largest ever recorded as being caught either by a particular method, e.g. rod and line, or in a particular territory, or both. For example, in the case of sea fish, commercial fishermen often take on lines and in nets larger fish than are recorded as taken by fair angling. Again, in Great Britain, Scottish and Irish pike are invariably larger than English specimens, and so forth.

Thus, though an angler may take a fish which does not break a national record, it may constitute a local record, or record for a particular water or just a club record.

Should an angler land a fish which he suspects might beat, or be in the region of, a national record he should get in touch *without any delay* with the British Record (Rod Caught) Fish Committee, the body which determines the identity of the species correctly and whether or not the specimen taken does constitute a record. To enable anglers to do this with as little delay as possible, because a fish loses weight after being taken from the water, the *Angling Times* arranges for the fish to be seen, weighed, and so forth, and the angler should therefore get in touch with this paper at Peterborough in Northamptonshire, either by telegram, or preferably by telephoning them at Peterborough 68345 up to 6 pm during the daytime, or 66809 or 5009 after 6 pm.

Since the first edition of this book appeared in 1967, the British Record (Rod Caught) Fish Committee earnestly considered the then record list. After considerable discussion they rejected a large number of the then recognized records and, ultimately, published a new list which left several places vacant.

All sorts of rumours flew around as a result of this: such as, did someone cheat, were so-called authorities mistaken, was the fish wrongly identified and if this were so was the wrongly identified fish then considered by the committee for candidature in its proper species? In match competitions there are many cheaters, leads put into fish, dead fish netted and put into the weigh-in, even fish caught earlier from other waters! The position was therefore extremely unsatisfactory, and still raises controversial discussion.

Because the list is continually changing I am not listing the record fish as set out by the Committee. However, lists are available on application to the official body or through angling papers.

Unfortunately, mere weight of the fish caught seems to be the criterion: this is wrong. The records should be decided not on the weight factor alone, after the other conditions as to identity, etc., have been satisfactorily decided, but on the tackle used in its capture. The breaking strain of the line is one factor which should be considered and also, in the case of saltwater fishes, whether it was taken through boat angling or shore fishing. Thus there could be two or three different record fishes of the same species according to the tackle or method used.

In the years which have passed since many of my angling books were published, I have seen my theories, thoughts, opinions, even descriptive phrases, taken up and used by subsequent writers of both books and articles – even to whole passages. I hope that my pioneering work in the abolition of treble and double hooks, which are both unsporting and unnecessary, will be taken up as eagerly by these other writers and by the Committee refusing to accept as legally caught for record purposes fish taken on these outdated and prehistoric pieces of equipment.

The introduction of *barbless* hooks into match fishing, both freshwater and saltwater, would be a great step forward in sporting angling and by adopting these as standard would be a reversal of the trend to use equipment which makes landing of fish easier by the unskilled and semi-skilled. It will revive true sporting instincts and not mean, as the conventional barbed hook does, of winching in small specimens as quickly as possible and cramming them into keep-nets or the bottoms of boats.

The ultimate disposal of the caught fish submitted for record purposes is of paramount *sporting* importance. There have, for instance, been cases where fish have been submitted for records which have been taken from their natural element, killed, and then buried! This surely outrages the rules upon which field sports are based. Because so many anglers are now inured to these events and accept them as normal, the new entrant to the sport must be the one to resist the present lowering of sporting standards and insist on the banning from specimen, record, and championship events the use of equipment such as double and treble (and on many occasions barbed) hooks which were items of pot-filling equipment used by prehistoric and aboriginal man!

I do not disagree with the record listing of large fish. But I do consider that the method of angling, the tackle used, the disposal of the 'body', do not receive the strict attention they should.

Specimen Fish

In addition to record fish, there are lists of specimen fish for particular waters. Every week awards (generally of fishing tackle) are given by national papers, and in particular the *Angling Times* gives one rod and two reels per week to those anglers who, in its opinion, have caught the best three fish of the week whether game, sea, or coarse specimens. The rules, in all contests, are that the fishes must be caught by fair angling by rod and line during the open season. Again various papers publish lists of 'Notable' fish, over a minimum weight.

Sometimes the angler may be puzzled to find that a fish of much heavier weight, in one species, may be passed over in a competition for a smaller fish of another species.

The reason for this apparent discrepancy is to be found in the fact that each fish is recorded in weight on a percentage basis of the record weight for each species. The term record weight does not necessarily mean national record weight. It is obvious that in national competitions the record national weight is the usual basis to work on : but for clubs and local competitions the norm is usually the record weight for that club, particular water, or region.

To express the weight of a particular fish in terms of percentage of a specified record a formula is used :

$$\frac{F}{R} \times 100$$

where F is the weight of the fish caught and R is the record weight of that species.

As several different species may be entered in the same competition the weight for F and R must be expressed in the same units : thus, where ounces come into the weight of either F or R, then both weights must be expressed in ounces, likewise if drams come into the picture, F and R must be expressed in drams.

For example, a gudgeon of 3 oz would count better, in the same competition, than a pike of 16 lb: each weight being based (in this instance) on the national record. A local record could alter the position if, for example, the national record gudgeon had been taken locally, but the local pike record stood at, say 18 lb. In this case the pike would be deemed the better fish.

It goes without saying that a fish should be weighed as soon as possible after capture on scales which can be certified as reliable, and at least two witnesses should be present when this is done. A problem may arise, especially in hot weather, when it is desired to retain the fish for examination by an expert. The fish may be preserved in a solution of formalin. This is easily made by adding a 40 per cent solution of formaldehyde to water in the ratio of 1 tablespoonful to 1 pint. A fish immersed in this solution will keep for several weeks.

Chapter 8

BAITS

THERE ARE innumerable baits which the angler may present to the coarse fish, and every angler seems to have his own special bait to which, logically or otherwise, he pins his faith. The most popular baits are bread paste, bread cubes, worms, gentles (or maggots), grubs, small live fish, small dead fish, stewed wheat, barley, hemp, elderberries, and so on.

Bread

Bread paste is made from fairly new bread. The crusts are cut off after which the bread is placed in a linen cloth and then placed in water. The cloth and bread are then removed and the surplus water extracted by twisting the cloth, after which the wet bread is kneaded into a paste. The essential thing to remember is that the hands must be absolutely clean when kneading or handling the bread. Motor car and motorcycle smells, such as petrol or oil, the smell of tobacco, cigarette lighter scents, must be removed from the hands, otherwise the bread paste will act as a repellent and not as a bait!

The paste is put on the hook after rolling it between finger and thumb until it resembles a pea. The hook is buried deeply within the dough blob so that the whole of the bend and point of the hook are covered. This is very important as I have often seen inexperienced anglers putting on the paste and showing quite an amount of hook point. They then wonder why fish do not seem to be lured to their basket. Some experts like to cover the whole of the hook, including the shank, with the bread paste.

There are various additions which may be made to the paste. Some anglers have been known to add a little cotton wool in order to make it stay better on the hook. Every angler has his own secret recipe and all sorts of oils and essences find their way into bread paste. However, I do not think ordinary paste, without any refinements, can be beaten, and when fish are taking the carefully prepared and scented dough of other anglers, they will just as well take the straightforward bread paste if presented properly.

Bread may also be made into cubes. This is made from the crust. The preparation is simple. The crust, about $\frac{1}{4}$ in. thick, is placed on a damp cloth, covered with another damp cloth and then pressed overnight between a couple of boards. The resultant sheet of bread can then be cut into cubes. Incidentally there is, on the market, the 'Milbro–Lesney' baiter presser for this purpose. It looks remarkably like an instrument of torture, the 'thumbscrew', but at only about 2s. 6d. presses the paste into a thin wafer which swells up to the proper size when in the water.

Bread crumbs, obtained from stale bread or by deliberately drying a loaf, slightly damped and then ground fine make an excellent 'cloud' bait. This, thrown into the water, remains in suspension for quite a time and attracts fish to the area : the main bait is then introduced into this cloud when the angler commences fishing.

Cheese

This is a good bait for chub. This may be worked up into a paste and may be used by itself or in conjunction with bread.

Maggots or Gentles

These are a popular bait and provide a whole industry in maggot breeding. It is not advisable to try and breed maggots oneself, in spite of what many authors on angling have written. It is a noisome business and can be a nuisance to one's neighbours. Maggot breeding is best left to the specialist 'factory'. Maggots bred commercially are advertised as plain, coloured, or natural. They may be treated with dyes to render them pink, yellow, red, or green. They may be advertised as liver bred, or ordinary, but regardless of all this they form a very expensive item in the angler's list. At 6s. to 10s. a tin, it is not uncommon for an angler to use £1 10s. or more over a weekend – and that's a lot of maggots. The small boy usually purchases 6d. of maggots in a tin, and does quite well. The real expense comes in the use of maggots as a groundbait: it is not the maggot on the hook which is expensive, but those thrown into the water.

The liver gentles are larger than 'carrion' maggots, and are a better proposition when the hook is going to be baited with one gentle only.

To bait a hook with maggots put the hook point through the fat end of the gentle: if two or more are being used the top gentle may be put on lengthwise and the others transversely, but the point of the hook must show through the skin of the last maggot.

Chrysalids

These are the next stage after the maggot: the grub becomes a chrysalis, brown in colour, before hatching into the blow-fly. The chrysalis may be used as a bait, particularly if it is a sinker or 'caster' as it is called in the North. Should one's supply of gentles become pupae then the chrysalids may be sorted by selecting them into floaters and sinkers. Some anglers discard the floaters or add a dust shot to make them sink.

Grubs

The wasp grub is an excellent bait, but it is a highly risky business smoking out a wasps' nest to try and get the grubs for angling with and not to be recommended! When wasp grubs can be purchased, however, they should be baked slightly before use to toughen them up to stay on the hook.

Grasshoppers

These are easily obtained during the summer months and

97

make a good bait for chub. As a dapping bait I doubt if they can be beaten.

Caddis Flies

These are sometimes found in streams, in great quantities. In other waters they are rarely found.

Meal Worms

I always think that these are horrible looking things! They are to be purchased from pet shops, rather than angling dealers, as they are used to feed the curious pets which people keep from time to time. They do make a good bait for roach and for dace, but are comparatively expensive to purchase.

Stewed Wheat and Barley

These are good baits, and, like hempseed, give excellent results because when a fish takes it generally results in a hooked fish. The grain can be prepared by soaking for 24 hours and then stewing it until the grains burst open. Sometimes the grain can be prepared in a vacuum flask. To use, bait the hook with a single large grain, and make certain that the point of the hook is showing through the soft skin of the grain.

Elderberries

Are very useful during the summer and I have known occasions when these are the only bait that roach have taken, in spite of the great variety presented by goodly numbers of anglers along the river.

Worms

A popular bait. Suitable for most fishes from roach to pike.

The most popular worms are brandling, red, and lob. These baits are easily obtained, though they may also be purchased from the tackle dealer. The brandling is found in manure heaps but before use should be, what is termed, 'scoured'. Scouring is done by placing the brandling worms in damp moss for two or three days before use.

The lob is the largest of our worms and is generally to be found in heavy damp soil, as well as in company with the brandling. Lobs may be trapped by placing sacking on the ground under which they will congregate, if it is kept damp. Lobs are also easily obtained on a damp night in the beam of a pocket torch.

There are two methods of hooking the worm. It may be caught underneath the skin or threaded on and worked up the hook until only a fraction of an inch remains free. For barbel, bream, and chub the tail only of the lob is recommended as an exceptionally good bait.

But, whatever worm is used, it must be lively. Dead and damaged worms are useless as hook baits and should be discarded.

Small Fish

Minnows, small roach and dace, bleak, may be used as live bait for pike and perch. Sprats, kipper, as well as other fish may, of course, be used as dead natural spinning baits, or legered whole for pike.

Whatever bait the angler uses, however, it is useless only making a small supply – nothing is more exasperating than to run out of bait. But, on the other hand, there is nothing more detestable than the fisherman who, through laziness or meanness, does not provide himself with either enough of or the right type of bait and who tries to cadge supplies from other anglers. These types of 'sportsmen' are on a par with the angler who fishes waters without permission, using as an excuse that he thought he could get permission from the bailiff when (if) he came along. Fishing on the cheap, by cadgers, may be satisfactory to them, but they are a waterside nuisance to decent fishermen and their activities do not come within the term 'sporting' angling.

There are plenty of bait materials available at home and in the countryside. What cannot be made up at home may be purchased readily. In the last resort, for emergency use, tinned or preserved baits such as minnows, elderberries, or paste may be bought from the tackle shop. Baits may be bewildering in choice; they are, however, simple to obtain and prepare and the true angler is identified by his attitude towards baits and baiting methods.

Part II

Fresh Water

GAME FISHING

Chapter 9

GAME FISH

THIS IS the glamour side of angling. The speckled trout of burn and loch, of white waters, stately chalk streams, and weir pools is the star of the angling world. The lordly salmon is pursued by comparatively well endowed anglers : but the trout and the sea trout are within the reach of most. It is the distribution of trout which presents the biggest problem to the angler.

My first fishing forays as a small boy were after trout in the becks and hill streams in the North of England, followed by excursions after them in Wales and Scotland. Consequently trout mean a lot to me. When I came to live in the South of England I was a little disbelieving about the sport to be had among coarse fishes : for me the trout meant the wilder country, the active pursuit of a fish, and coarse fishing looked slow and uninteresting. It was only after trying out coarse fishing that I found its subtle fascination. But trout and coarse fishing have nothing in common – they are different arts, each requiring different skills and knowledge. Now, though it may sound heretical (for to me trout fishing is a wonderful sport!) I consider that the good roach fisherman is the better angler in so far as feel of the fish and reaction is concerned : his skill is really superb. The trout fisherman, however, inherits the thrill of the hunter. He stalks his fish personally and, unlike most coarse fish, especially the chub, the trout is full of fight from hooking until the end. I often go coarse fishing, but if I were forced to give up freshwater angling and limit myself to one angling excursion per year, then it would be after the fresh run sea trout in a Scottish river.

I think this is because there is such a difference between the speeds attained by game fish as opposed to coarse fish (the pike excepted). The brown trout has been timed to swim at a speed of 23 mph, the pike at 20. Compared with these speeds the barbel at 11 mph, the perch at 10.5 and the carp at 7.5 mph are loitering.

Again, probably because I am the hunter type, I prefer to fish for game fish for the logical reason that I like to eat them : in consequence the catching of large numbers of them is of no importance : unlike the match fisherman who must needs catch as many as possible. One or two trout and I am quite happy ! I have yet to taste something better than the small burn trout freshly taken from the water and fried in butter over a fire lit when the fishing started.

Game fish have different close seasons from coarse fish. In Scotland the annual close season for trout is from October 7th to March 14th following, both dates inclusive. In England and Wales the statutory close season for trout (excluding rainbow trout) runs from October 1st to the last day in February.

The close season for salmon in Scotland varies according to the river and may run from October 1st on some rivers and be as late as December 1st on others. A lot of rivers open the season for salmon during January, others remain closed until as late as April 14th. In England and Wales the statutory close season for salmon runs from November 1st to January 31st, both dates inclusive.

The game fish in the United Kingdom are divided into salmon, sea trout, brown trout, and rainbow trout. In the past there have been many varieties of trout written about, such as bull trout, white trout, and so on. Today it is agreed among anglers that the four species named constitute the salmon family of game fish in British freshwaters.

Typical of the weights game fish, taken in British waters by fair rod and line angling, can attain are shown by the following recorded specimens :

Salmon 64 lb. This was caught on the River Tay in 1922 by Miss G. W. Ballantyne.

Sea trout 22 lb 8 oz. This was caught in the River Frome in 1946 by S. R. Dwight.

Brown trout 18 lb 2 oz. This was caught in Loch Garry in 1965 by K. J. Grant.

Rainbow trout 8 lb 8 oz. Caught in 1924 at Blagdon by Lieut.-Col. J. Creagh-Scott.

There is a correlation between weight of the fish and its length, if in good condition, and as an indication of size, enabling the angler to assess quickly the weight of a fish roughly, without scales, the following table might assist:

Trout	length	9 in.	weight	5 oz
		12 in.		12 oz
		15 in.		1 lb 7 oz
		20 in		3 lb 7 oz
		24 in.		5 lb 15 oz

Salmon	length	30 in.	weight	11·57 lb
		33 in.		15·4 lb
		36 in.		20 lb
		40 in.		27·4 lb
		48 in.		47·4 lb

Trout vary remarkably in their coloration, size, and habits according to the different waters in which they are found and this has probably given rise in the past to the many so-called variations in the species.

The colour of the fish depends a lot on its surroundings. A trout which frequents waters with a weedy, muddy bottom will often be yellow tinged whereas a trout taken from a rocky or sandy area will have a richer bluish colour.

In small and shallow streams they run rather small, but in deep lakes and lochs trout can attain a large size. Indeed the older trout taken from large waters is sometimes mistaken by the beginner for the salmon, and it is a little confusing to count rays in dorsal fin or scales from the rear of the adipose fin to the lateral line as they may be identical in both species. One sure identification point is the fact that in the salmon the corner of the mouth is level with the rear edge of the eye whereas in the trout the mouth extends back farther.

To add to the confusion in the beginner's mind there are several local names relating to game fish which he should learn so that he can identify them from such descriptions.

SALMON

Bagot, sometimes also called a baggit. This is the hen fish which though entering a river for spawning does not release her eggs.

Grilse, a salmon which, after spending one winter in the sea, has returned to fresh water.

Kelt, a salmon or sea trout which, after spawning, is returning to the sea. The fish is in very poor condition.

Kipper, a salmon which has been in fresh water for some time and is now about to spawn.

Fry, a young fish after emerging from the egg. It starts life with a yolk sac attached to its body which it gradually absorbs and ultimately becomes a very small fish an inch or so in length. The next stage of development is known as the Parr.

Parr, a fish between the fry and stage when it begins its journey to salt water.

Peel, a salmon *grilse* which weighs less than 2 lb.

Pink, a salmon parr.

Shedder, a hen fish which, after spawning, is returning downriver to the sea.

Slat, a kelt.

Smolt, a salmon which has completed the parr stage and is commencing its journey to the sea. At this stage it turns silver.

SEA TROUT

Bull trout, this was a name once given to trout found in Northumbrian waters, believed to be a separate species, but now known to be a common trout.

Finnock, Phinock, Herling, Hirling, Whitling, Scottish
   names for sea trout grilse.
Kelt, spent fish, after spawning, as in salmon.
Peal, a West-country name for sea trout.
Sewin, a Welsh name for sea trout.
White salmon, sea trout.

TROUT

Boddagh, dollaghan, Irish names for trout found in Lough
   Neagh.
Bull trout, see under sea trout.
Ferox, large predatory trout found in deep lakes and
   lochs.
Gillaroo, an Irish lake trout.
Slob, the name given to trout which, becoming silver in
   colour, live in estuaries.
Sonaghan, Irish name for trout found in Lough Melvin.

Trout are very accommodating fish : they are widely distributed in the streams and waters of the West country and
in the North of England, Wales, and Scotland. They are
easily reared and many reservoirs and 'lodges' hold these
good sporting fish. In the North of England the art of fly
fishing for trout is not confined to the rich; many mill
waters as well as water board reservoirs hold trout which
may be fished for on an annual ticket. In the South of England the chalk streams and the few waters which are given
over to trout are more expensive to fish. There seems to be
a basic difference in approach to angling between Northern
and Southern anglers : the one sees waters holding game
fish : the other prefers to see the waters stocked with coarse
fish : neither are wrong : it is simply that there are not
enough fishing waters to go round and the wicked way in
which industrialists and local authorities have polluted our
fair rivers and streams is a sad reflection on our so-called
progressive society.
   There are several ways of fishing for trout. Chief, of
course, in the eyes of the élite is dry fly fishing, on the chalk

streams, followed by wet fly fishing. Dry fly fishing is a cult in itself and, unfortunately, it has attracted a lot of snobbery. Contrary to general belief dry fly fishing is not the most skilled method of angling, but there is no harm in letting the enthusiast believe it is so : it saves a lot of argument!

Spinning and worming are other methods by which the trout may be lured to the landing net.

Most reservoirs and lakes confine the angler to fly only, but on some of the larger lochs, the very big trout are rarely taken on the fly and the spinner has to be used : even so, the biggest trout are to be taken after dark on a large hook baited with lobworms.

Whatever the method of fishing used, the angler must become acquainted with the haunts and habits of the fish. Trout vary in feeding habits according to : (a) type of water in which it is living, (b) nature of the feed, and (c) size of the fish. Trout take flies and insects from the surface, but also feed at mid-water and on the bottom. In general, however, it may be stated that the larger the fish the less likely it is to take insects from the surface, it is more likely to feed at mid-water and on the bottom, tending to be predatory. However, this generalization is incorrect. During the period when flies hatch out and cover the streams in large numbers, the big trout will feed readily on them : and this occurs again during the May-fly season, or 'Duffer's fortnight' as it is called. During this period large trout will take the fly from the surface though during the remainder of the season they will remain obdurate bottom feeders.

In small streams, particularly hill burns, the trout run very small indeed and will readily take the fly. Indeed, on some lochans I have had trout taking the fly so readily that they appeared to have gone mad in an effort to become hooked. But, again, this readiness by small burn trout to take the fly can just as suddenly disappear when the fish become dour and will not take.

The best times for trout fishing are morning and evening. The term 'rise' denotes the surface feeding fish and there is surely no more exciting sight than the rise of trout in some Northern loch, the rings on the water spreading out in every direction, coupled with the great heart-stopping splash as a big fish eagerly takes the evening fly.

However, the novice must not assume that the breaking of the surface of the water indicates a 'rise' and that, therefore, the trout may be angled for. Sometimes a trout will 'tail'. A tailing trout is one which is searching for small aquatic creatures with its head down and it is the tail which breaks the water surface. 'Bulging' is another term, referring to the disruption of the water by a fish which is swimming after and taking a larva or nymph rising to the surface. But 'smutting' is the term he will come to hate. This refers to trout rising to swarms of tiny gnats or midges, too small to imitate by the artificial fly, and when fish are 'smutting' they are very difficult, if not almost impossible, to catch.

The dry fly angler selects and stalks a particular fish and has to present his lure accordingly: but in lochs the trout are often to be found in shoals and though on calm days the dry fly may be used, in general the wet fly, in strongly contrasting colours such as the Zulu or Butcher, is a better proposition.

In addition to brown trout, some waters are stocked with the rainbow trout. This is not a native fish, but was introduced from Canada and has received a good reputation as a sporting fish. It rises very freely to the fly and has proved to be a fairly easy fish to rear. The rainbow trout usually spawns during February and March, but recovers fairly quickly and is in good condition by July. It differs from the common trout in size, running much smaller, it has smaller scales, a shorter head and is differently coloured. The gill covers and a broad line along the mid-side of the body are coloured carmine. The back is very dark and has black spots as also the head, tail, and fins. Sometimes all the fins are tipped white, though this is usually confined to the ventral and anal fins.

The sea trout are known as sea trout parr when they are

about the size of a minnow but become smolts when they are preparing to take to salt water and become silvery. The next stage in development of the sea trout is when the two foremost fins become bright yellow, and in some parts of Scotland they become known as the 'Yellow Lug'. On returning from the sea to fresh water in a beautiful silver colour they are known as 'Finnock' and 'Herling'. Their next stage in life is the sea trout and after maturing and spawning they become kelts.

The salmon must be distinguished from trout and sea trout if the beginner is not to take a fish illegally. The commonest mistake, intentionally or otherwise, is that of confusing the salmon parr with a brown trout. This is an unnecessary error because there are the following points of difference. The parr has a sharply shaped head, that of the trout is blunt. The parr has a V-shaped tail, that of the trout is almost straight. Again, there are dark marks along the body of the parr which have been described as 'fingermarks' – these are absent in the case of the trout.

It is illegal to take or be in possession of parr, sea trout 'yellow lugs', and kelts. The kelt salmon is a long, lean, poor-looking fish. The bright red of the gills of the healthy fish has become dull and crimson, and the fish, sluggish and a poor fighter, is usually toothless. The kelt is, however, limited to the spring season and is not encountered later in the year.

There is also a territorial distribution of the fish. The brown trout remain fairly high up the rivers and streams, but the sea trout and the salmon gradually drop downstream until the migration time into salt water arrives. Sometimes brown trout will drop downstream and live in an estuary and in these circumstances they become known as 'slobs' or 'slob trout.'

Grayling

This is a sporting member of the salmon family but, as explained in an earlier chapter, it does not breed during the same season as the other game fish.

Some anglers look down upon the grayling, maintaining that it does not fight as well as a brown trout. One has to admit that the dash and fierce resistance of the trout is absent in the grayling, but when hooked it does a lot of diving and boring and this, coupled with the fact that the mouth of the grayling is delicate, requiring light handling when playing, means that skill is required to basket it.

Unlike the trout, which is often 'put down' by the artificial fly, the grayling will continue rising so that the angler is given the opportunity of bettering his cast to a particular fish. But the grayling is a rapid riser and requires quick reactions from the angler, otherwise the fish will be missed.

Unlike the trout which prefers to lie singly, the grayling moves about in shoals, so that when they are taking there is a better chance of making a decent catch.

But the one great point in favour of the grayling is the fact that they come into condition about the end of July and are to be caught until the end of December when they really are in their prime for eating at that time.

The size of the grayling will vary from water to water, and run larger in the South than in the North, and though grayling of up to 4 lb are said to take the fly, in the main worming and spinning accounts for the larger specimens. Most grayling caught are about 1 lb in weight.

The record stands at 7 lb 2 oz caught on the River Melgum in 1949 by Mr J. Stewart.

The grayling does not have the same hue as the trout, but is a silvery fish, deriving its name, probably, from the greyish marks on the sides of the mature fish. The young grayling gradually become duller in colour as they mature. Another peculiarity of the fish is the distinctive odour it gives when taken from the water, rather like the smelt does, resembling the scent of wild thyme and from which it derives its Latin name of *Salmo thymallus*.

Some anglers aver that the grayling destroys the young of trout and try to clear them from their waters: this is founded on mistake of the facts. Grayling breed in different parts of the water from the trout and this assumption of the grayling killing off the trout fly is based on the fact that grayling breed in a different season. After all, trout will also devour small trout.

Chapter 10

FLY FISHING

AS THE angler will have learned in Chapter 6 there are different methods of fly fishing, but the mechanics of casting remain the same. I have dealt with the difference in rod required for dry fly fishing and wet fly fishing and I think that at this stage one should deal with the cast.

Just as the modern skier learns to 'dry' ski, to get used to movements and get his correct muscles working, so the beginner in fly fishing is advised to fish 'dry'.

The best way to begin is to find a large field, car park, or other open space where one can practise. And it is essential that the beginner have plenty of room *behind* himself as well as in front as will be seen later.

First of all fit up the rod, reel, and line and at this stage dispense with the cast and fly. Take up your position with your back to the wind but do not, at this stage, place any target, such as a handkerchief, on the ground at which to aim. The object of this first lesson is to get to know the feel of the outfit and to recognize that *it is the rod which has to do the work*, not the angler.

The wrist and forearm are the portions of the angler which are used, not the shoulder.

Stand easily, facing the right direction. Relax. Hold the rod in front of yourself, at an angle of about 45°, with its own length of line hanging down from the top ring. Now pull out enough line with the left hand so that another 8 or 9 ft have been pulled off the reel but hold this taut, ready to let it go. Gently raise and lower the rod tip allowing the free line to work out so that the line lies on the grass in front of you.

Grip the rod firmly with the thumb on top and pointing along the rod and with the first finger below.

Now pull another yard of line off the reel and hold it taut but ready to release. Waggle the rod to and fro, backwards and forwards until you can feel the line held in the left hand trying to go from your hold. When you can feel this yard or so of line pulling, let it go and you will find that you have actually 'shot' that portion of line. Keep on doing this until you have six or seven yards of line out.

Perhaps here we should recapitulate and go over the mechanics of the cast step by step (Fig. 14):

1.   With line extended out in front and with the rod held at about the 10 o'clock position strip some line from the reel and with thumb and forefinger of the left hand. Hold in a loosely coiled position.

2.   Draw in slack line by bringing the left hand back and then start swinging the rod tip upwards. This must be sufficiently fast to bring the line into the air and whip it upwards and rearwards.

3.   Just *before* the rod reaches the vertical or 12 o'clock position the wrist comes into action and bends so that the rod tip goes slightly past the vertical.

4.   At this point pause.

5.   The rod tip will now bend backwards to approximately 1 o'clock position behind you and the line should straighten out, floating in the air behind you.

6.   At this moment start the forward cast, driving the rod tip *forwards*. It is imperative that the tip is not driven downwards.

7.   When the rod reaches midway between 10 o'clock and 9 o'clock positions the wrist is stopped and this halts the rod tip. At the same time the line begins to straighten out and the coil of line held in the left hand will signal that it is ready for release. Let this spare line go when it will shoot through the rod line guides.

It is essential, before you carry on any further with the practising, that you are able to keep the line (up to 36 ft at least) fairly straight in both directions, forward and behind.

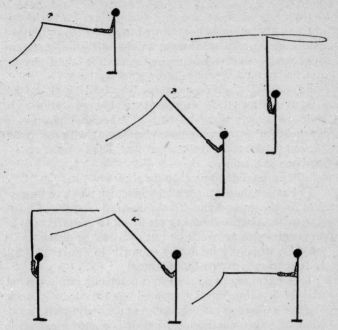

14 Making a cast with the fly. (*Left to right – upper*):
(*a*) Ready to make slow motion lifting of line off the water
surface. (*b*) Accelerated motion carrying rod up and back
and slightly to right. (*c*) Rod upright – here a slight pause
is made to allow the line to travel backwards and stream
out behind the caster. (*Left to right – lower*): (*d*) Fast movement by straightening forearm bringing rod tip forward
to next position. (*e*) Line shooting forward and rod movement slowing up. (*f*) Rod lowering ceases – line allowed
to follow tip on to the water

This is termed 'false casting' and must be thoroughly mastered.

The beginner must beware of being in a hurry in this practice. If the line is not allowed to straighten out before the forward cast is made there will be a 'crack' like that of a stockwhip expert performing at a circus, and any fly attached to the line will be thrown off.

It is advisable, after the cast has been made, with the line lying in a straight line before one, that the rod is allowed to continue slowly forward until a horizontal position is reached. This is to ensure that when fishing with the fly on, the tail fly drops on to the water first. The fly must always land before the line.

Now is the time to practise for accuracy.

The angler should place a handkerchief, plate, or sheet of card on the ground and from a distance of about 8 yd to start with, practise dropping his fly on to the target. As he progresses with accuracy he can increase the distance. Remember, when dry fly fishing one casts to a particular fish and accuracy is extremely important.

The next thing to do is to start practising into the wind. And the first time this is attempted you are due for a shock. Then practise false casting and accuracy casting with a side wind, and also practise left hand. It is a good idea also to practise casting near bushes and other obstacles. You will find obstacles a-plenty when fly fishing the waters and it is advisable to become thoroughly proficient before wetting a line.

Dry Fly Fishing

This is practised to perfection on the chalk streams, but is not limited to them by any means. The water in chalk streams is invariably gin clear, and the banks of the rivers are usually low. This means that anglers are easily visible to fish in the water and, as they lie invariably with their heads upstream, they must be approached cautiously from downstream. The clearness of the water means that the fly must be presented naturally, and furthermore, must approximate as closely as possible the particular species upon which the fish are, at that time, feeding.

Now in dry fly fishing one has to cast to a particular fish, which means that either the fish has to be seen, or the rings from his rise on the surface. The best fish to stalk is the continuously rising fish; he really is on the feed and not so likely to be scared off by a clumsier than usual approach!

Before, however, just approaching the water and looking for a fish, it is advisable to know where the trout are likely to be. Fish like to lie in the neck of pools, in runs, and either in front of or behind large stones or boulders. They are also to be found in the tails of pools.

On approaching such places the angler should keep himself as inconspicuous as possible, not show himself high on the bank nor clump about noisily.

It follows that the angler must stalk his fish as carefully as possible and take advantage of such natural cover as there is. I have known really keen anglers lie prone on the ground and cast, successfully, from that position.

The first effort at casting a fly to a fish may well end in failure. The fly must be put well above the fish so that it floats down to him and the fish, if it takes, must be given ample time to turn its head downwards before the strike is made. Again, drag on the line must be avoided.

Drag occurs when the currents in a stream flow at different rates, as, for example, when a fly is cast across the water into a slow current but a faster flowing current in the middle of the stream carries the line into a big curve. This results in the fly suddenly being dragged across the water at an increasing speed and this results in a badly scared fish which will not take again for several minutes. The way to overcome drag is to try to give more line to the fast water and this is done by casting too far and then checking the line just before the fly drops.

So remember, study the current before you make your cast.

The fly must float on the surface (Fig. 15) and remain visible all the time, and to ensure this special flies have to be made or bought. Before fishing, the fly should be treated with a touch of oil or similar substance to keep it waterproof. Between casts it is usual to make two or three false casts to get rid of any excess moisture and dry the line, cast, and fly.

Incidentally, it is advisable to make a couple or so of false casts after oiling the fly, to get rid of the superfluous oil.

However, let us assume that the cast has been properly delivered, there is no drag to scare the fish, and the fly is floating down to the feeding trout. As the fly floats down the slack line should be gathered in gently and the take

15 A winged fly : this is fished 'dry'

carefully watched for. Do not strike, or lift the rod tip when you see the water surface boil, as to do so will merely snatch the fly out of the trout's jaws. The breaking surface is caused by his head so you must wait, calmly or as calmly as possible, give the fish time to start downwards and then just *slightly* raise the rod. This so-called strike will drive the point of the hook home. Note that the strike is leisurely, in keeping with the nature of the water. If fishing wet fly upstream in a rushing burn, then the strike is rapid, in tune with the mood of the water.

So far, dealing with the dry fly, I have referred to approaching the trout from below and casting upstream. But there are times when, due to natural obstacles, such as bushes overhanging the lie of the fish, it is not possible to fish upstream : downstream casting is therefore called for.

First of all, to avoid coming with the vision of the fish it is essential to cast from as far a distance as possible. The cast should also allow for any possible drag on the surface. And if you have cast and missed the fish, gently draw the fly into your own side of the stream and try not to disturb him, otherwise that will be the only cast you will make to him.

So far so good. The attention of the novice will have been directed at the fish, but whether casting upstream or downstream, there is one thing the fly fisher must do : he must glance behind him before casting to see whether or not there are any obstacles likely to catch up the fly on the backward leg of the cast!

From time to time the angler will get caught up in a tree or bush. If it is not possible to get at it to free the hook then do not try to reel it in. Take up the slack on the reel and then waggle the rod tip about to try and unhook the fly. Sometimes it is possible to reel in until the fly is at the rod tip and then unhook it from the branch or bough in which it is caught.

Wet Fly Fishing

On some waters this is forbidden, but this does not mean that it is an undesirable method of angling. It arises from a long time past when wet fly fishing was conducted downstream with dragging lines, spoiling the angling for the dry fly man. Wet fly fishing is, today, recognized as a skilful and artistic method of taking fish (Fig. 16).

Wet fly fishing is generally divided into two methods – upstream and downstream. Many anglers regard upstream wet fly fishing as the best of all methods. This form of angling is carried out among highland rivers and burns, or streams with steep high banks, rocky walls, waterfalls, rapids, and deep, still pools. Fishing from the bank is generally unproductive as fish are easily scared off by the sight of a figure waving a rod high above them. Wading becomes the method of approach, and wading from behind, Red Indian fashion, is carried out slowly and quietly up the river or stream. During this approach, and from his experience in knowing where trout are likely to lie, the angler searches out the fish by means of his fly or flies. The fly is cast only a short distance ahead and once it is in the water it has to travel downstream at the same speed as the water current. This means that as the fly travels towards the angler he has to gather in the loose line. The line must always be tight so that the angler can feel the slightest knock or touch of a fish. As the fly approaches the angler the slack line is drawn in by the left hand whilst the right wrist slowly raises the rod tip. The whole exercise must be smooth and sure. At the same time the angler must concentrate his gaze on the spot where the fly is, watching for

16 A hackle fly : this may be fished 'wet' or 'dry'

the slightest movement or flash of the fish taking it. Whatever is signalled to the angler, he must strike at once, a mere twitch of the wrist being sufficient. So quick must be the angler's reaction to the take that it can only be described by an angling friend of mine as 'Striking when the fish makes its mind up to take the fly!'

Downstream fly fishing is a matter of necessity rather than choice, but in Scotland in big waters downstream is often the only method by which the fly may be fished. In fast swollen waters it is sometimes only possible to fish downstream. Downstream is easier for the beginner as the current does his work for him, but many fish are missed because the hook is more liable to be pulled from the jaws of the trout. It goes without saying that the angler should make his cast from well back from the edge of the bank, thereby keeping out of sight of the fish as much as possible.

Sea Trout

The best places for finnock or herling are in the estuary, the best method is to fish the falling tide across and down the stream, and the best times are in the late evening. Sea trout are better fished for in higher stretches of the river and the hours immediately after sundown are the best. The really deep pools will often produce the best sea trout at their tail and a large fly cast into such a pool, into the darkness, often brings the thrill of a splash and the runaway attempt to escape by a strong fish. You don't have to worry about striking with a sea trout: he attends to that for you. Both wet fly and dry fly may be used, or special flies such as the 'terror' (Fig. 17) and 'tube fly'. The 'terror' is a two- or

17 A 'terror' fly for trout and seat trout fishing

three-hooked lure with a streamer dressing – favourite flies for the sea trout being 'The Alexandra' and the 'May Demon'.

To enable the novice to form an opinion as to what flies he should have in his box for trout, finnock, and sea trout fishing, the following list might be of value:

Trout Flies

Dry Flies

March Brown	April
Pale Olive	April, June, July
Iron Blue	April and May
Grannom	April
Blue Dun	April
Olive Quill	April
Wickham's Fancy	April, May, June, July
Greenwell's Glory	April

Alder	May (late), June, July
Black Ant	May
Red Spinner	May
Medium Olive	June, July
Sedges	August, September
Olive Dun	August, September

Wet Flies

March Brown	March/April
Greenwell's Glory	March/April
Coch-y-Bondhu	March/April
Blue Upright	March
Wickham's Fancy	April
Grannom	April
Coachman	May
Tup's Indispensable	May
Black Gnat	June/July
Alder	June/July
Red Ant	July
Iron Blue	July
Red Palmer	July/August
August Dun	August/September
Cinnamon Sedge	August/September

Sea Trout

Teal and Red
Silver Butcher
Dunkeld
Teal and Green
Silver Doctor
Butcher
Zulu
Black and Blae
Grouse and Claret
Tup's Indispensable
March Brown
Ginger Quill

So far we have considered fishing for trout and sea trout in moving waters. The angler must now turn his attention to loch and lake fishing.

As lochs can be very large the angler has first of all to try and find out where the fish are likely to be. The first problem is to ascertain the direction of the prevailing wind. Then, having ascertained that, the angler may safely assume that the flies will be blown on to that end of the water more than elsewhere and should provide good feed for the fish. Secondly he has to look at the topography; the contours of the ground about the loch as well as the contours beneath the surface of the loch.

Waters entering or leaving the loch, islands, shallows, must all be noted: and the items referred to become even more important if the fishing is going to be done from a boat. The presence of deeps and shallows determines where the fish are likely to be, and especially if fishing large Scottish lochs, variations in the depth of the water due to droughts, heavy rains, and so on must be understood. From my own experience in the big lochs I have known a swell on the water of several feet, and if fishing from a small boat in the proximity of rocks, or over shallows, damage may result to the craft if it is brought over such underwater features.

From the bank the angler can determine a rough picture of the loch or lake. A steep cliff or hill will, for instance, usually indicate that there will be deep water: this is not invariable for I have known steep cliffs terminate in a shallow going some distance into the water. A flat, peaty, or gravelly shore generally indicates a similar flat, shallow area in the water.

Islands, especially if wooded, generally give a good angling spot and if there are several islands together, they are generally, though not invariably, connected by an underwater ridge and it is along these ridges or 'roads' where fish are likely to be found.

Artificial reservoirs are generally constructed with a shallow at one end, from the natural hillside, terminating in a steep man-made bank, generally stone covered. It is usually from the steep end that the bigger fish are taken.

For fishing from the shore the best conditions are those when there is a gentle breeze. This puts a ripple on the water and helps to hide both the angler on the bank and the line on the water from the fish. Though long casting may be necessary on some reservoirs, as a rule when loch fishing from the bank long casts are not necessary because the fish are generally lying close in. Again, the angler should try to cast across wind when fishing from the bank. Unfortunately the shores of a loch curve about a lot and even when fishing from the same shore the angler may find that, occasionally, he will have to fish into the sun. This makes it extremely difficult to see the fly and the aid of polarized glasses should be sought: if polarized glasses are not carried by the angler, then a pair of sun glasses may help him. The best time for fishing a lake or loch is after sundown.

Fishing from a boat is done, not by rowing about the water, or anchoring the boat in one place, but by turning the craft sideways on to the wind and allowing it to drift before it.

The angler fishes pretty much in the same way as from the bank but there is no necessity to fish with a long line. It is true that fly fishing from the boat covers more water, but when a fish is hooked it brings additional problems. First of all every endeavour must be made to keep the trout from going under the boat. If the fish does so the cast will probably be broken and the fisherman should never attempt to pull the fish back from under the boat via reel. Instead he should point the rod tip round either stem or stern and gradually play the fish to windward.

Above all, the angler should keep still and not try to go from one end of the boat to another as if he does so he is liable to capsize the craft. When two anglers are fishing from the same boat they should do so from either end and it is an act of sporting courtesy when one angler has a fish on, for the other to reel his line in until his companion has either boated or lost the fish.

Talking and noises on the bottom of the boat are prohibited. Water carries sound and vibrations which easily put the fish down.

Sometimes the speed of the boat, drifting down wind, may be too great and it is advisable then to put a small drogue or sea-anchor over the side to slow down the drift. Alternatively a large stone on a rope may be put over the side. If either of these appliances are used, then the angler must be careful to see that when playing a hooked fish he keeps it away from the ropes.

The boat may be rowed back into the wind and the angler may cast his flies from the stern so that they are trailed behind it: this is sometimes successful, and I have found flies such as the Zulu very effective for this purpose. This method does, however, savour to me more of spinning than fly fishing.

If the angler is hiring a boat complete with boatman then he can depend upon the local knowledge of the latter to give him a good chance to come to terms with the fish. If the angler is visiting a water for the first time, and for a limited period, perhaps during a holiday, it is very possible to use up all of one's fishing time trying to find the right spot under certain conditions. With a hired boat and boatman the angler is assured of a short cut towards this objective. He is a very important person, the boatman, and it pays the angler to note very carefully the weather conditions, the strength and direction of the wind, the ripple on the water, the position of the sun, and then watch how and where the boatman places the craft. One can learn more in one day doing this than spending a whole week at the waterside trying to find the things out for oneself.

The Duffer's Fortnight

I have mentioned this peculiar phrase earlier and the angler may well wonder what it signifies. The term is given to that time in the early summer when the May Fly suddenly appears. This is a beautiful insect with wings rather like a dragon fly, but with a helpless fluttering flight. During the Duffer's fortnight they appear in scores of thousands and after a brief existence, culminating in mating, the male falls dead upon the surface of the water and the female, after laying her eggs, also dies. The surface of the water during Duffer's fortnight is soon dotted with thousands of dead and dying May Flies, then known as 'Spent' flies. In its brief existence the fish rise steadily and gorge on the May Fly, so that a couple of weeks after Duffer's fortnight they have become so gorged they refuse to look at any bait offered to them. During the Duffer's fortnight, however. the fish rise so well that the beginner will remember the experience all his life.

The May Fly is invariably fished dry and the imitation fly is dressed as nearly as possible to correspond to the natural insect.

Chapter 11

SPINNING FOR TROUT

THE PURIST regards any other method of taking trout than on the dry fly as inferior, and almost poaching. But this is a narrow view which, fortunately, is becoming rarer as the purist becomes better educated in matters pertaining to angling!

The equipment is very much the same as spinning for coarse fish; a short, light, and powerful rod and a good fixed spool reel make a good combination.

With the fixed-spool reel the angler is able to cast farther distances than the fly fisherman can, and water which is normally beyond the reach of the fly fisher can be covered easily by the spinner. This does not interfere with fly fishing and often accounts for the large fish, feeding near the bottom, which has become what is known as a 'cannibal'. In actual fact all trout are cannibals, but the term is given to the large predatory fish.

Natural minnow makes a good, if messy, spinning bait, and I think that the artificial 'Devon' about 1½ in. in length, in a variety of colours, gold, silver, blue and silver, brown and gold, with both right- and left-hand twist, so that the lures can be alternated to keep twisting out of the line, is a better proposition.

I have also used the ABU 'Hi-lo' pike plug, and found that spun from a boat in deep lochs, the larger trout take it readily. A good lure is a spoon bait, generally fished in large lochs fairly deeply, with an irregular recovery.

When recovering the 'Devon' the speed should be increased as the lure approaches the shore, to keep up a natural imitation of a small fish trying to escape into the shallows. If fishing in fast running waters, the minnow should be heavier than for lake fishing.

If fishing for sea trout or finnock the cast should be down

the current, recovering the lure upstream. If, however, one is spinning for them in an estuary the better method is to cast slightly upstream.

Bright days are better for spinning than dull days and, unlike fly fishing, the late evening is seldom profitable for the spinner.

Some anglers like to 'troll' their lures: this consists in rowing a boat with the spinner over the side and the rod in a rest. This is not really angling at all but merely towing a hook around the lake or river. It is not to be recommended because it is possible for the lure to pick up a snag, such as a sunken bough, and perhaps damage the rod: the least it can do is break the line, causing the loss of line, cast, and lure. If the rod is not held by the angler or put into a proper rest when trolling it is possible for even worse things to happen. I remember an angler on Esthwaite Water doing this and as he passed me on the bank his rod gave a twitch then went overboard! The lure, a large spoon, had got caught up in a bunch of weeds and pulled the rod overboard. It was fairly deep water and it cost him an entire fishing day trying to recover it: furthermore, by the time I had finished angling (moving farther along the bank because he was disturbing the water) he had not recovered the lost articles, nor did I ever hear that he was lucky in getting them back!

The tactics when fishing for game fish with the spinner are the same as when fishing for coarse fish: big lures for big fish. I must caution care in handling the lures with their treble hooks: though a single can easily be removed from a finger or ear, the treble is a different thing entirely and needs medical assistance to do this.

Chapter 12

WORMING FOR GAME FISH

'GOOD HEAVENS! Do you mean you actually use a *worm* to catch trout?' I remember this expression of horror when I was telling a dry fly friend of mine, who fished reservoirs only, about upstream worming for trout in Scottish burns and Welsh streams. I could see that he thought I was beyond the pale: would be capable of shooting a fox, and nodding to a lady instead of raising my hat; worming for trout, indeed!

However, let me assure you that I did manage to convince him that this was not something not done. Furthermore I was able to get him to try out upstream worming in a North Wales stream and what is more, he enjoyed it!

First of all, let me explain that the type of waters on which worming is carried out are the smaller, very rapid streams, which vary immensely in depth. These rapid rises and droppings in water level vary from a thin trickle, 1 or 2 in. deep, to madly rushing, brown torrents.

When waters are low, during the dry summer months, the fish are not inclined to rise for the fly and trying them with the feathered lure in these conditions is a waste of time: upstream worming becomes the only practicable method.

The technique is to wade upstream, and this may mean walking up stretches which barely cover the angler's feet, the water being so shallow. It will seem impossible for fish to be found in these conditions. The rod must be about 9 to 10 ft long, and rather stiffish – approximating a dry fly rod. A fly line with a cast terminating in either a single hook or a two hook 'Pennell' tackle is used, with a lively red worm thereon.

The line is cast ahead of the angler with the slack line gathered in by the left hand as the bait travels back to him.

When the lure reaches the angler he swings it forward again, again searching out another run or eddy.

The worm is unweighted and no float is used. The worm is sunk below the surface of the water so that the angler cannot watch it like a dry fly. The secret of watching for the sign that a fish has taken is by keeping one's attention on the two or three feet of line immediately below the rod tip. The tell-tale sign of a take is a quiver in the line and all that it is necessary to do is to lift the wrist to drive the hook home.

It is a matter of timing – and timing is gained only by experience. The big secret is to strike very soon, though with a single hook this may result in leaving the worm tail with the fish.

A trout can lie in between 2 and 3 in. of water and if you catch, or swing your worm into such a shallow run and seek out the places behind stones, you are likely to have success.

Worming for trout may be carried out downstream : but is not quite so successful. I have fished clear water downstream with the worm but this has been a matter of necessity. The occasions have been when I have followed a burn up into the hills to its source, fished the small lochan usually found there, then continued down into the next valley. I have had to fish the descent downstream. The secret is again to keep the line tight so that as the lure tumbles about between the stones the slight knock by a fish is felt. The strike is slower than when fishing upstream as to strike quickly will mean drawing the hook away from the fish's mouth.

There is an easy, almost poaching method of basketing large trout and that is swimming a worm downstream, either with float or rolling leger, during a flood. When the water level is high and the colour brown and thick, a worm swum down in such conditions often brings a large trout. A good place for this sort of fishing is where a burn empties into a loch.

I have mentioned large trout taken on a leger at night.

These fish often refuse to look at flies and are difficult to come to terms with a spinner: a bunch of lobs, legered after dark, will often bring a cruising monster in. This is not really going after game fish in a sporting manner, but it is done by pot hunters for whom a good sale to restaurants and hotels is more important than the art of angling.

Part III

Sea Angling

Chapter 13

SEA ANGLING

DURING THE past decade there has been a tremendous growth in the numbers of sea anglers. This has been due, in the main, to the limited number of fresh waters available. Furthermore, the increase in transport facilities means that many anglers can get to the coast who, hitherto, had to fish nearer home. Nowhere in Great Britain is the coast too far to travel to and certainly the freshwater angler often travels greater distances in his angling quests.

The old myth that sea angling was crude : that the tackle resembled telegraph poles with a hawser for a line : that it was unskilled and that 'chuck it and chance' was the golden rule, has well and truly been given the lie. Firstly, sea angling is as skilled as freshwater angling. The fisherman must know the topography of the sea, he must understand the tides (which ebb and flow twice a day), he must understand the fish he seeks so that he has to be at the right spot at the right time with the right bait and the right tackle. The beginner may have luck, but the consistent angler has to have skill, coupled with knowledge.

There is a popular misconception abroad that sea angling consists of sitting in a motorboat, trailing a handline with a lot of feathered lures attached, travelling back and forth over a holiday bay, bringing in some luckless mackerel. This happens at holiday resorts every season – but it is not angling.

Sea angling consists of the correct and sporting use of a rod and line, hooks, and reel.

Sea angling has the following advantages over freshwater fishing :

1. There is no close season.

135

2. There are no licences to buy or permits to obtain, except the occasional small pier toll.

3. It is not necessary to join a club to fish.

4. The species which may be caught are well nigh endless: and vary from pouting of a few ounces to shark and skate over the hundredweight.

5. The angler may fish as light as the roach enthusiast, or battle with big game fish, such as shark and conger, which will test his strength and courage as well as his tackle.

6. Night fishing, so often prohibited in coarse fishing waters, is not illegal for the sea angler. In fact much of the best sea fishing is done at night.

7. Whereas the freshwater angler cannot examine the bed of his river or lake, the sea angler has the opportunity twice a day when the tide uncovers the shore, to examine its nature. To note its contours, its peculiarities, and most important of all to collect his bait from the very spot in the very form on which the fish have been feeding and present it to the fish, on a suitable hook, in that very place where the fish will be looking for it.

8. Angling equipment is, in the main, cheaper to purchase for the sea angler than for the freshwater fisherman.

As for the fishes themselves, the mackerel, caught on suitable tackle, is every whit the equal of the sea trout for sporting possibilities: the grey mullet can test the skill of the best roach angler: the bass and pollack can equal the thrills of the perch and pike angler: the skate, the tope, the conger have no equal in fresh water.

Sea angling consists of many different aspects of the sport. Fishing may be carried out from the beach, when it is known as shore fishing. The angler may fish from gentle sloping beaches or from precipitous cliffs (as much as 100 ft or more above the sea), from slippery weed-covered rocks over a boiling surf, from a jetty, or holiday pier: from large or small craft, close inshore or a score of miles out to sea. Indeed, sea angling is a general term for half a dozen different angling sports carried on in salt water.

The British Record (Rod Caught) Fish Committee have a new list of sea fishing records, which they alter and re-issue from time to time. The current list is always available either on application direct to the Committee or from angling journals.

Sea fish can run from a matter of a couple of pounds weight or so in the case of Garfish, to almost 900 lb in the case of the Tunny. Fish have been recorded for many, many years, but with the great number of anglers fishing today, there is considerably more interest in both record fishing and in specimen hunting for one species. By and large, however, it can be stated as a general rule that sea fish taken by the boating angler will run larger than fish taken by the shore or pier angler. Also, the man who fishes in deep water, well offshore, has a greater chance of bagging large specimens than the man who fishes from a small craft only a few hundred yards offshore.

The picture of angling is changing, however. Anglers tend to go further and further afield in motor-craft, and often go well out of British waters. So much so that there has had to be a restriction on the recording of fishes outside these areas. Again, the building of power stations along the coast has also altered the nature of the angling. Whereas cod in certain areas were deemed to be giants at 25 lb, those same waters, heated through the power stations, are now attracting and holding fish of 40 lb or more! No wonder the record list has to be revised from time to time!

World angling records of saltwater game fish are recognized and based on the strength of the line used. I most earnestly represent that for British saltwater records, the same procedure should be adopted. After all, a 20 lb pollack taken on 30/40 lb breaking strain line, isn't half as meritorious as one taken on lines of half that strength!

I see no reason, too, why the type of hook should not be taken into consideration. There is absolutely no reason why a new class of records for barbless hooks should not be introduced and gradually replace the existing ones!

One thing I must protest against is the growing tendency of sea anglers to indulge in competitions which result in trying to boat as many fish as possible. This is not in the true spirit of angling and I cannot too strongly emphasize the revulsion I feel when I see fish taken for the sake of taking them. There used to be a symbol of class warfare in our society, still visible now and again, which refers to the shooting man as slaughtering pheasant, or grouse, for the sake of the bag, or big-game hunting for the sake of a head. The angler who goes out merely to win a competition and fill a boat or a keep-net at all costs is in the same category as the American 'buffalo hunter' – the sight of piles of dead fish, such as tope, on a jetty or beach, upsets the non-anglers, is a waste of fish life and a denial of conservation principles, and, furthermore, provides ammunition for the anti-sporting bodies and 'do-gooders' who are only waiting an opportunity to ban all forms of field sports, *including angling*, altogether.

In the following chapters, I have set out brief descriptions of the sea fishes which the British sea angler is most likely to encounter. If I have referred to record weights at all, it is merely to indicate sizes to which it is claimed the various species can run.

Chapter 14

SEA FISHES

SEA FISHES are generally divided into two types, (a) round fish and (b) flat fish. Most sea fishes fall into the first class, being conventional in appearance, but the flat fish, of which the flounder and the plaice are members, do not, contrary to general belief, swim on their stomachs like the round fishes, but swim on their sides. Thus, with a flat fish it is incorrect to speak of a dark back and a light belly: it should be referred to as having a dark upper side and a light lower side.

Flat fishes commence their lives as normal round fishes, with their eyes on each side of their head but gradually, as they grow, they turn on to one side and thereafter one eye works through the body and ultimately they both appear on one side! Fish are identified by whether their eyes are on the left or the right, in addition to colour distinction of course. The dab, flounder, and sole, for instance, have their eyes on the right: the turbot and the brill have their eyes on the left.

Angler Fish

This is a peculiar, even ugly, species which rarely falls to rod and line, and even then solely by chance for I have never heard, known, or read of any angler who has fished specifically for it.

The Angler Fish lives on the sea-bed and is therefore usually taken only on legered bait, though sometimes a very deep bait which has been driftlined may take one. It gets its name from the peculiar and very long dorsal first ray which overhangs its enormous mouth. The tip of this ray ends in a 'lure' and this is tantalizingly swung about to tempt other, smaller, fishes within the cavernous jaws.

Another feature of the angler fish is the fact that it changes its colour scheme to match the sea-bed which is its habitat. It also has adornments of ragged weed-like fringes of skin round the lower jaw and on the body. The body tapers abruptly to a small tail and is scaleless. The pectoral fins are used by the angler fish for walking about on the sea-bed, for it is a very poor swimmer. The teeth point backwards and are in two rows in the jaws. There are sharp spines round the eyes and the head is immense and flattish.

It is distributed fairly generally round our coastline but cannot be described as common. Sufficient to state that it is rare enough a capture to excite comment and a small crowd whenever one is landed by a 'lucky' angler.

Bass

This fish goes by many different names. It is called basse, white salmon, sea perch, sea dace, salmon bass, schoolie, sand bass, king mullet, white mullet, gapemouth and gapie, according to locality.

This attractive and grand sporting fish belongs to the perch family and, in common with other members, is equipped with a spiny dorsal fin. This, when erected, can inflict a wound upon the angler careless in his handling of the fish. The colour is attractive, the back is dark blue which gradually gives way to a silvery white belly and sides. The fish, when the dorsal fin is not erect, has very much the appearance of a salmon and thus it is easy to understand why it is sometimes called salmon bass or white salmon. The head is rather larger for the body than in the freshwater perch and the mouth is very large.

The fish weighs from a few ounces, when it is termed a school or a shoal bass, to about a stone. Average weight of mature bass appears to be in the region of 4 to 5 lb, but this, again, varies from locality to locality, and fish taken in the north are often larger than south-western bass. The majority of fish taken weigh in the region of $1\frac{1}{2}$ to $2\frac{1}{2}$ lb. A bass over 8 lb is a very nice fish, a 10-pounder worth shouting about, and a 12-pounder will never be forgotten!

The average bass taken by the shore angler will be smaller than that caught by the boatman.

The bass inhabits southern waters, and though large bass are taken in the north, they are comparatively scarce there. In Scotland, however, they are rare enough not to be worth angling for specially. From Cornwall to Suffolk, round the South coast, there are excellent bass grounds. The Welsh coast also provides good bass angling, with Menai Straits yielding fine specimens. On the East coast there is good bass fishing north to Scarborough, but it tails off after that.

Bass are to be found, chiefly, on rocky coasts and estuaries, but they are also to be found over sandy shores. Indeed fish over 12 lb in weight have been taken off Ryde pier in the Isle of Wight, and that is essentially a sandy stretch of coast.

Bass are taken all times of the year. Once upon a time they were fished for in the summer months, but now bass often figure in specimen fish awards after September, the month in which they used to leave our coasts. The best periods for bass angling are during the spring tides, and early morning and in the late evening.

They may be taken on a variety of baits and by any number of methods. They will take the fly, they may be spun for, and float tackle, drifting, legering, and paternoster will all account for bass in every size.

The best bait for bass is the living sand-eel fished on a driftline, but other good baits are dead sand-eel, live or dead prawn, fish lasks or lasts, shell-fish, green crab, soft crab, cuttle-fish, lugworm, ragworm, and mussel. But all these baits, and others, need not be too fresh as bass like their food a trifle 'high'.

As bass have big mouths it follows that large hooks, certainly nothing under size 1/0, should be used.

Bream

There are three species of Sea Bream which are likely to be caught in British waters. These are Red Bream (sometimes called Common Sea Bream), Black Bream, and the Becker.

Red Bream. This fish has a variety of other names and may be called Brim, Red Gilthead, Chad, Chad-bream, Barwin, Gunner, Brazier, and Carp or Sea Carp.

This species seems to vary its locality from season to season, occasionally appearing in one district for a while and then disappearing. It is fairly common round the Cornish, Devon, and Southern Coasts.

The Red Bream season extends as a rule and depending, of course, on climatic conditions, from the end of May to the beginning of October, with June being probably the best month for successful red bream angling. As is the case with sea fishing in general, the larger specimens are taken when boat angling.

Angling methods which are successful are paternoster, leger, and driftlining. The most useful baits are sand-eel, lasks of fish, ragworms, and mussel. Size 1/0 hooks are recommended. As may be expected the sea bream family are not unlike the freshwater bream in general appearance; they are rather handsome fish with deep bodies. They are equipped with a spiny dorsal fin, like that of the perch, and this runs almost the entire length of the back.

Black Bream. This is also called the Sea Bream, the Baker, and the Old Wife!

In physical characteristics it is very similar to the Red Bream but is rather localized in its distribution, being found mainly off the coasts of Dorset, Hampshire, the Isle of Wight, and parts of Sussex. It is a summer visitor and is a shallow water fish. Boat fishermen are most successful with the Black Bream and best methods for taking are driftlining with at least a 5 ft trace. Float tackle trotted down the current also accounts for a good number of these fish. Ground baiting is an essential item if the angler is to be successful.

The Black Bream is apt to change the depths at which it feeds, but, by and large, they are to be found about 4 ft off the bottom.

Baits used are lugworm, mussels, sand-eels, and thin strips of herring, mackerel, or bream.

Becker. This is the third and rather unimportant member of the family of sea bream. It is sometimes called the 'Braize' in some districts. It is very similar in appearance to other bream but has a blue back and silver sides and belly. Unfortunately this rather attractive fish soon changes colour after being taken from the water and turns almost black.

It is poorly distributed round our coasts but often appears among pout and is caught from midsummer to mid-autumn.

The becker feeds at varying depths from mid-water to the bed and the most successful rigs to use are paternoster and leger. Again, driftlining can be successful. The best baits are strips of oily fish, such as herring, mussels, and ragworm.

Though the becker is not, as a rule, specially fished for, it is a worthwhile species to catch as it is strong and gives a good fight. Moderately strong tackle is required. Incidentally, the becker is really first class as a table fish, far better than either of the other sea bream.

Coalfish

This is a good sporting fish, giving sport not only to conventional sea angling but to the fly fisherman. It has a lot of different names, which vary from locality to locality. In Cornwall it is termed the rauning-pollock, in Scotland it rejoices under the titles of saithe, sillock, saidhean, gerrock, cudden, cuddie, herring-hake, coalman, suyeen, while in Yorkshire it is identified under the name of billet, blue-back, or parr. In different parts of the country it may be identified under the names bil, black pollack, black-jack, bleck, blockan, billiard, coalsey, coal-whiting, colmey, cooth, comely, gilpin, glassan, glashan, glassoch, glossan, green cod, green-pollack, green-whiting, gull-fish, harbyne, lobkeeper, lob-keeling, piltock, podling, prinkle, sethe, seypollack, stenlock, graylord, and dagie or dargie.

The coalfish can vary in size from 2 or 3 lb (the cuddy of Scotland and the billet of Scarborough) to over 20. The back is very dark green (note the names of green cod, referred to earlier) though sometimes it may be more blue than green. The belly is white. There are three dorsal fins and the lower jaw has a barbel. The average weight of coalfish caught in British waters on rod and line is about 4 to 5 lb.

Coalfish are to be caught from about the middle of May until the end of October, depending upon climatic conditions. Most shores hold coalfish, though Yorkshire and Scotland seem to provide the best coalfish angling. They are often to be found near rocky or mixed ground and seem to prefer weedy shores to others. They hunt the herring fry in shoals and the best angling methods for these fish are fly fishing, spinning, float fishing, driftlining, and paternostering. Legering is not usually a very successful method as the coalfish is more partial to a moving bait. Paternoster tackle is only moderately successful.

The living sand-eel is by far the best natural bait to use, with dead sand-eel a good standby. Other good baits are peeler crab, lugworms, lasks of fish, and live prawns. Of the artificial lures used the 'Porosan' sand-eel is easily the best, followed by the ordinary rubber sand-eel. Almost any shining lure can be used to spin for these fish and I have frequently caught them by using naked hooks with a portion of foil from a milk-bottle cap twisted on to them.

Hook sizes from 1/o to 4/o are to be recommended for coalfish, though for small members of the family size 8 may be large enough. The coalfish is not usually recommended as a good eating fish, and, like the mackerel, must be eaten as quickly as possible after landing. The coalfish, along with the pollack and the dogfish, is that great standby of the English fish and chip shop – the 'Rock salmon', that mythical fish which is served so often!

Cod

Probably the most important fish so far as man is concerned. The cod family, like the freshwater carp family, is a large one. The cod, whiting, pollack, coalfish, pout, haddock, ling, hake, and the torsk are some members of this vast and useful family of sea fishes.

This fish is really too well known to need a description. It may vary in colour from locality to locality. Yellow, brown, red and speckled specimens are found and the best eating cod are those with the reddish tint. The codling is generally used to describe fish of up to about 4 lb in weight. However, in some districts the term codling would be used to describe a fish under 20 in. in length, and a fish about 30 in. long would be termed a sprag. There are other descriptions coupled with weight and size of fish, such as half-cods and cods. Cod can run large. Fish of up to 20 lb and over are not uncommon.

The best fishing months for cod are winter months. January and February generally bring the best cod angling, and the sea usually runs from September to March.

A ground feeder with an enormous mouth and a catholic taste for food, the cod needs large hooks and large baits. The best rig is leger and the paternoster a good second. Baits recommended are sand-eel, squid, mackerel, herring, lugworm, ragworm, sprats, soft crab, but almost any fresh bait will do.

Conger Eel

This big fish is to be found all round our coasts, wherever the sea-bed is rocky. I, myself, when writing *The Complete Sea Angler*, classed the conger as a British Big Game Fish and that lead seems to have been followed. Specimens over 100 lb in weight have been landed by commercial fishermen and the present record, for fair angling with rod and line, stands at 84 lb. The female fish is larger than the male and the average size of a large conger taken by anglers is perhaps in the region of 30/35 lb.

Conger may be caught from jetties, piers, and rocks, though conger taken under these conditions will rarely be very large. Slippery rocks, in the night-time. though good places for conger hunting, can be very dangerous. Even a comparatively small conger eel is a very powerful and determined fish and the excitement of a fight, in the dark, on weed-slimed rocks, could well result in the conger getting the better of the angler and precipitating him into the sea, with fatal results.

The best conger fishing is done from boats and the best conger grounds are deep holes and old wrecks.

They prey on other bottom fish and are usually angled for on strong running leger tackle baited with fresh squid or cuttle. If this bait cannot be obtained then in order of importance the angler should use mackerel, pilchard, herring, or sprat. The bait must be absolutely fresh as conger are deterred by anything which is slightly 'off'.

The hook must be attached to a wire link because the sharp teeth of this fish will prove too much for nylon. Personally I would recommend cord for the trace, rather than wire, because the soft material is not likely to make the conger reject the bait by taking something hard into its mouth. A cord tracer is easier to cut through than wire when removing the hook from a *dead* conger: it is not recommended to attempt to remove the hook from a live one, unless one wishes to lose a finger or even hand!

In addition to wire or cord trace there should be two or even three swivels as when a conger is hooked and being played he not only pulls and battles but spins deliberately. These swivels help to stop the line being twisted on recovery.

The hook for a conger must be large and strong.

Leads can prove to be an expensive item from their constant loss and a piece of scrap iron or a large nut attached to the tackle by a piece of cord makes an excellent sinker. The cord need only have a few pounds breaking strain so that if the weight becomes caught up among rocks, or in a portion of a wreck, it is torn away without loss of hook, line, or trace.

Conger fishing is no sport for the timid, especially at night, and it can prove a dangerous fish to land. A conger, even a dead one, can inflict a nasty wound with its powerful jaws and sharp teeth and any attempt to remove a hook from a conger's mouth is downright stupid unless the fish is well and truly deceased. There are several anglers, with missing fingers, who can testify to this horrid fact. Stout shoes or boots must be worn when conger fishing as bare feet, or feet clad in plimsolls or wellingtons, are simply asking to be mauled. A reasonably sized conger can tear the sole from an ordinary shoe! The best way to secure a conger is to handline him ashore or into the boat and drop him into a sack tail first. A blow from a powerful conger could knock an angler overboard. A conger can be stunned by a blow from a cudgel over the vent : but the only certain way, after stunning the brute, is to sever the spinal cord with a sharp knife.

A conger makes pretty good eating and fried conger steak is almost as good as halibut.

Dab

This is a flat fish, sometimes also called the sand dab. It is generally found over sandy shores and therefore its general colour scheme is sandy on the upper side, flecked with brown and orange. A lot of the smaller dab are almost transparent. The skin is rough on the back and the mouth is at the end of the snout. The eyes are on the right. The dab is fairly well distributed and though the record dab stands at over $2\frac{1}{2}$ lb the average dab caught by rod and line would seem to be in the region of 12 oz. The dab is a bottom feeder and therefore bottom tackle is best, with paternoster beating the leger. Dabs are small fish and require fairly small hooks, about size 6. The best baits are lugworm, ragworm, mussel, and uncooked peeled shrimp.

Tackle should be light and the strike should be slightly delayed because the dab likes to mouth the bait first before taking.

Flounder

Another member of the flat fish family. This is similar to the dab with the eyes on the right but the colour of the back is greenish or brownish, sometimes greyish. The skin on the back is smooth and covered with mucus.

The flounder is ubiquitous, even to be found in fresh

water, much to the surprise of many freshwater bottom fishermen.

The flounder is in good condition during the winter and early spring but is reputed to be best for the table during the midsummer months. Angling methods include paternoster and leger, together with float tackle, as the flounder will take in midwater and I have successfully caught flounder on a spinning bait when after other fish.

Soft crab, lugworms, and ragworms are good flounder baits. There is also a good method of fishing known as baited spoon and also wander fishing.

Garfish

Here is a sporting fish both unusual in appearance and in its fighting tactics. The garfish is not often specifically fished for, but is often taken when fishing for mackerel. This is probably the liveliest fish ever to be encountered by the sea angler for it is a veritable aquatic acrobat. It is a beautifully coloured fish with sides of silver and a greenish-blue back. The average garfish runs to 18 to 14 in. in length and has only recently been included in the list of record fish. In appearance one can appreciate why the garfish has been called the sea-needle, for its body is long, slim, and almost eel-like. The tail is forked and very streamlined, and the dorsal and anal fins are set well back. The mouth is equipped with a long snipe-like bill. The roof of the mouth is extremely bony. Garfish make an excellent bait.

On the table they are excellent eating, but the cook has to overcome his or her first reaction of distaste when seeing that the fish has green bones!

When a garfish is hooked he leaps from the water, swims in mad rushes in all directions both away from and towards the angler, and generally does everything possible to confuse him. One moment he will stand on his tail, the next bore deep. When boat fishing one has continually to pass the rod tip from end to end.

Other names for the garfish are : gorebill, longnose, gar-pipe, sea-needle, needle, needle-fish, sword-fish, spearling, green bones, green-bane, and snipe-fish.

Gurnard

There are several gurnards or gurnets. There is the Red Gurnard, or soldier or cuckoo gurnard: the Sapphirine Gurnard, or tubfish (sometimes called red tubs and smooth-sides) and the Grey Gurnard (also known as gowdies and crooners).

The appearance of a gurnard cannot be confused with any other species. They have large square-shaped heads. Their bodies taper rapidly to the tail. There are two dorsal fins the forward of which carries spines. The ventral fin is almost oversize for the size of the fish. The gurnards also have six feelers projecting from the throat which the fish uses to find food on the seabed.

Distribution is as follows:

Red Gurnard – south and west of England and Scottish coast.
Sapphirine Gurnard – the East coast.
Grey Gurnard – widely distributed.

The gurnards are chiefly bottom feeders, though some-times they may be taken in midwater. The principal methods to use to catch them are leger and paternoster and the best baits, in the following order, are fish strip, soft crab, mussels, sea worms.

The spines of the dorsal fin can give the angler a nasty cut if he is careless when handling a gurnard, and gurnard skin makes an excellent material for artificial sea flies.

The Sapphirine Gurnard is the best on the table as it may run up to 5 or more pounds in weight and, stuffed and baked, is a first-class dish.

Hake

This is a member of the cod family, but minus the barbel on the bottom jaw which is such a point in other members of this family. The average size of the rod-caught hake is about 5 lb but fishes of up to a stone are not uncommon. The hake is a long, slim fish and has a spiny dorsal fin. He is ferocious and it is inadvisable to try and extract the hook from his mouth while he is still alive, otherwise lacerated fingers may result.

The hake is very popular in the North and is distributed well in Scottish and Irish waters. The season for hake is in the winter from October to February and night-time is the best time to go after the hake. They are predators and they like to hunt the herring shoals. A large, single hook with a wire trace, baited with a whole herring or pilchard and a line to match in strength, is best. During the beginning of the season hake may be found near the surface but as winter progresses they should be sought lower in the water. They are chiefly the quarry of the boat angler though the shore fisherman may occasionally encounter them.

Haddock

Another member of the cod family, common enough in the fish markets as not to merit a description. The haddock is not a big fish and the average caught by rod and line sea anglers is about $2\frac{1}{2}$ lb. Commercially taken in nets the haddock can run to tens of pounds.

The haddock is a good sporting fish and is a shoal fish: so that if the angler gets his first fish, he may pretty well be sure of others to follow. It is fairly well distributed with the greatest concentrations off the east coast of England, as well as Scottish and Irish waters. The haddock is a winter fish. It is a greedy and ferocious taker and the best tackle for him is the paternoster rig with a lugworm baited hook, size 1/0. Squid is a good bait, as also oily fish strips, and some anglers are very successful with mussel.

John Dory

This is a bizarre fish, ugly but strangely attractive! The body is deep and compressed. The dorsal fin is large and contains long, sharp, dangerous spines. The anal fin is also equipped with these spines. The overall colour of the fish is olive-brown, suffused with a golden-yellow tinge. There are black spots behind the gill-covers which legend says are marks left by St Peter's fingers (a legend, incidentally, also given to the haddock, neither of which fishes are to be found in the fresh waters of Israel). The John Dory is a sluggish fish and is caught more often accidentally. Most of these queer fish are in the region of 2 to 4 lb. It is also capable of making a grunting sound when taken from the water.

Ling

This is a powerful and ugly fish, a member of the great family of cod. He is found fairly well distributed round the coast and is a winter fish. The ling is voracious and large hooks and strong lines are required. The same baits and angling methods are required for ling as for cod.

Mackerel

This fish is almost too well known. This is the handsomest of British sea fish with its bright blue-green iridescent wavy bands on his streamlined back. It is not a large fish, but size for size, fished for on light tackle, it is the gamest fish in British waters, fresh or salt! Its distribution is fairly general but the greatest concentrations are in the south-west waters.

The season for mackerel extends throughout all the year, but the best months are from April to September and March and April are the best months for table qualities.

Angling methods are various. The mackerel feeds at any depth from surface to bottom and may be fished for in any of the conventional ways. Spinning with light tackle, with a bright spinner, or a rubber sand-eel is an excellent way of taking these fish. I use a light spinning rod with a closed-face reel, with a 2 lb breaking strain line and a wagtail bait for mackerel, and a good and successful combination it is! A good way of mackerel fishing, and getting the best sport from the fish, is to use light trout tackle for them, fishing a fly, the Alexandra for preference. A piece of mackerel skin cast and worked like a fly is also a successful method. Trailing long lines of gaudy feathered lures behind a boat is *not* angling for mackerel, it is merely catching fish.

Of baits – strips of mackerel are the best! But mackerel are pretty catholic in taste and will take ragworms, entrails of fish, sand-eels, and squid.

One word of warning – the mackerel, lovely to look at, fun to fish for, excellent on the table, must be eaten promptly, certainly within 24 hours of capture, otherwise it goes 'off' and becomes dangerous to eat.

Grey Mullet

There are three grey mullet in the British list. These are the thick-lipped, thin-lipped, and golden mullet. They all have thick bodies, small mouths, and short broad heads. Their coloration is silver with dark strips running lengthwise. There are two dorsal fins, the front one carrying four spines, and the tail is forked.

The mullet is fairly well distributed.

The season for mullet is during the summer and during the midsummer months they feed mostly on the surface. They have soft mouths, so that a hook is soon torn from them, and they are suspicious and shy of strange baits. They are hardest to catch in harbours, but easier to catch in open water. Surface fishing after ground-baiting the area is often a successful way to catch them. Light float tackle, with ragworm, macaroni, peeled shrimps, or bread paste, is a good method and I have found the best tackle to be a light quill float, a 6 lb b.s. line, a number 9 hook with four small white ragworms on, and a split-shot about a foot above the hook.

A mullet takes the bait cautiously. He may suck in the lure and blow it out two or three times. When float fishing the float must be set to cock at the slightest bite, and this is where the mullet fishing approximates roach fishing. But here the resemblance ends for a mullet may run anything from 2 to 15 lb and he makes a frantic rush when hooked.

Plaice

Another well-known flat fish, running much larger than either dab or flounder. The average sea angler will take plaice from 1 to 4 lb, but the commercial fisherman will take them up to 10 lb. The plaice has an overall hue of brown on top with very well defined red or orange spots. There are several hard knobs in a line behind the eyes.

The plaice is widely distributed, and is to be found over sandy bottoms, fairly close inshore.

Angling methods are similar to when fishing for dab and flounder but with stronger lines and larger hooks. When landing a plaice the angler must watch out for the sharp spine on the ventral fin which can give him a nasty gash when unhooking the fish.

Pollack

A typical member of the cod family, but without a barbel on the lower jaw. This fish rejoices in a whole set of different names such as: lythe, whiting-pollack, laithe, greenling, skeet, whiting-cole, and greenfish.

The fish is generally green or bronze in hue which grows lighter towards the lateral line where it is marked with gold. Belly and undersides are white with a yellow tint. The lower jaw protrudes. The pollack is widely distributed and is to be found chiefly off the rocky coasts. It also frequents clumps of weeds. Evening and early morning are the best times for pollack fishing.

When a pollack takes the hook he does so most definitely! Even a small pollack is a powerful fish and strong tackle is necessary. If the water is fairly shallow and weedy and the pollack tears off in a first mad rush and manages to reach the bottom there is little the angler can do about it. If, however, the water is deep and free from weeds, then the angler may let the fish run and use the length of line and drag on the water on it to tire the fish. If the water is shallow that first rush must be stopped – the fish has to be held.

Later summer and early autumn are the best times for the pollack fisher. Angling methods are the same as for the coalfish and the pollack will take at all depths from surface to bottom. Fly fishing, with the cuddy fly, legering, drifting, paternosting, and spinning are all equally effective at bringing pollack to the basket.

The average rod-caught pollack is about 4 lb but the angler must be prepared to deal with fish of up to three times that weight. Strong tackle and a gaff are essential items in the pollack hunter's list.

Pouting

Another member of the cod family which gives a terrific amount of sport to the general sea angler. There are other names this fish rejoices in, chiefly rock-cod, Bib, whiting-pout and blind. It has a short, deep body and carries a dark patch on the pectoral. The fish has a barbel on the lower jaw and runs to about 1 lb in weight. The pout is a winter fish and the best months for catching the larger pout are December and early January. It is a widely distributed fish with a preference for rocky ground or weedy area. Old wrecks frequently make good pout grounds.

The pout is a bottom feeder and this means that leger and paternoster tackle are necessary. Large rag, strips of fish, mussels, lugworm are all good pout baits.

Scad or Horse Mackerel

This fish is often taken by holidaymakers and mistaken for the mackerel! It also goes under the name of moss-banker. It does resemble the mackerel superficially, but is not very good on the table. It is a bigger fish than the mackerel and often runs over 3 lb in weight. If fishing for scad the angler should use light but strong tackle with small hooks. A strip of mackerel is the best bait, but it is a catholic feeder and nothing comes amiss. They are sporty fishes, even if disappointing on the table, and give hours of fun to the pier angler. Unless they are going to be used as bait, or as a table experiment (and don't say you were not warned!), they should be returned to the water as quickly as possible after capture.

Sharks

Not very long ago the thought of shark fishing in British waters would have been regarded as the product of a deranged mind. Today shark fishing is very much a part of the sea angling scene. There are shark clubs and shark fishermen round most of our coasts and though some of it does approximate the holiday mackerel angler, in that the novice is taken for a trip, provided with tackle, and helped catch a small shark, the fact remains that this is a growing sport attracting both male and female anglers to its ranks.

The British sharks include the *Tope*, which is abundant on the south and east coasts of England as well as the Irish Sea. These fish may run from 20 to 70 lb, with the female being the larger of the species. From the culinary standpoint the tope is useless.

Special equipment, with wire traces, is necessary and a stout rod and reel for tope, as for other shark fishing.

The *Blue Shark* is bluish in colour and has a long pointed snout. It runs from a few pounds in weight, not much larger than a dogfish, to well over a hundredweight.

The *Porbeagle* is a faster fish than the blue shark and runs to a larger size. It is found chiefly in our western waters. Its chief characteristic is the very disagreeable odour it gives off, so much so that porbeagle shark are rarely taken aboard the fishing craft, but towed behind.

The *Thresher*, also known as the sea fox. This shark is very agile and has an enormous tail fin, equal to the body of the shark in length. It is extremely active and leaves the water in enormous spectacular and dangerous leaps. The prospect of a large thresher crashing on to a small craft has, before today, caused the timid angler to cut the line and let the fish escape. An angling friend, who was a professional photographer on a national newspaper, used to recall how he went to take pictures during a foray after shark. 'I'll never forget,' he said, 'seeing that fisherman playing a shark ten feet in the air!'

The *Mako*. This is a ferocious shark from tropical waters which is a visitor to British waters. Probably because our waters are colder than its usual haunts it has not, so far, been found to be a man-eater here! The present record for Mako shark taken in British waters stands at over 498 lb and that is a lot of fish.

For shark fishing a stout rod is necessary, with a large game reel. At least 300 yd of stout line, with a breaking strain of 40 lb or over, together with a steel trace or leader of 18 ft length and a large hook are the basic requirements.

Skate

The common skate is a large fish. It runs to about 100 lb and more, though smaller specimens of about 20 lb are commonly taken by shore anglers. The boat angler must always be prepared to deal with large skate. As will be realized this fish is very strong and can use its weight, strength, and water pressure on its wings to become well-nigh immovable.

Rays

There are several of these in British waters, chief being the Thornback and the Sting Rays. The latter has a sting for a tail which has a poisonous spine on it, and this means that great care has to be taken when handling it. Ray will take most baits, but it must be clean and fresh. Stout rods with at least 30 lb breaking strain line are necessary. A ray or skate which takes to the bottom takes a lot of moving be-cause it manages to clamp its great body down to the sea floor and with the pressure of the water on its upper sur-face it takes an awful lot of strength to move it. The rod and the tackle must be in good condition because once the angler has managed to lift such a fish it has to be pumped to the surface. The skates and rays probably account for more smashed tackle than any other species in our coastal waters.

In common with many other sea fishes the skate is capable of inflicting serious injury on the angler who is careless in his handling of the fish. The male reproductive organs in this species contain a pair of 'claspers' which have bones which are razor keen. If handled wrongly these can make a deep and dangerous cut and most professional fishermen cut these 'claspers' off when the skate is landed.

The skate should be gaffed in the wing for landing and if it is over 40 lb in weight, then two gaffs are advisable, one in each wing.

Whiting

From the giant skate and rays we turn to a much smaller, though none the less valuable, sporting fish. This is a small member of the cod family, and together with the codling, is often the sole reason for many anglers going sea fishing during the winter.

The whiting, silver in appearance, is beautifully streamlined. It does not grow to a large size, indeed the record stands at 6 lb, and unfortunately often weighs ounces. On average a whiting of 12 oz to 1 lb is regarded as a good specimen. But in Northern waters whiting grow to a larger size.

The whiting is plentifully distributed but the sea-going angler has a longer season for during the very cold months the whiting retires to deeper waters.

A word of warning to the careless angler: and how often these warnings must appear. Tiny though it is, the whiting is equipped with very sharp teeth which can tear or cut clumsy fingers trying to retrieve a well-taken hook.

The whiting is a bottom feeder and leger and paternoster are the best method to employ to bring him to the basket. A driftline worked near the bottom is also productive. The tackle may be fairly light and the hooks about size 7 or 8. Soft crab, mussels, ragworms, fish strips are all excellent baits for the whiting is a catholic feeder. I have also used whole sprat and often landed a whiting who has attempted to swallow a sprat nearly as big as himself!

The Wrasse

There are three main species of wrasse which frequent our shores: the green wrasse, or ballan wrasse: the cuckoo wrasse, or blue-stripe: and the conner wrasse or gilthead.

All are fishes which haunt the rocks, all are beautifully marked with coloured marblings on their deep bodies. They are excellent sporting fishes for they fight strongly and when hooked make for rock crevices. Fairly strong tackle is necessary and as the line is often drawn over and around the sharp rocks the angler must continually examine his cast and line for signs of fraying and wear.

Wherever there are wrasse, the angler is likely to encounter pollack, so the wrasse angler must be prepared for an encounter with that species.

Angling methods include bottom fishing and, my own preference, float fishing. Lugworm, ragworms, soft crab, strips of fish are all good baits.

Unfortunately though the wrasse is a colourful fish and a good fighter, it has an unenviable reputation on the table. Wrasse caught should therefore, unless required as bait, be returned to the water, or given to some lobster fisherman who likes to use wrasse flesh as bait in his pots.

Chapter 15

MORE SEA FISHES

IN ADDITION to the fishes mentioned in the previous chapter, there are several other species of sporting sea fishes which the angler may encounter. Some of these are not specially fished for, some are landed by accident, and some, like the weever, are extremely dangerous not only to the angler but to others who wade or swim in the sea.

Distributed widely in deep water, and a popular sight on the fishmonger's slab is the *Sole*; this is not often landed on rod and line as it is mostly a night feeder. The *Turbot*, too, is a member of the flat fishes, and though specimens figure occasionally in the lists of prize-winning fish, they are usually caught by accident when the angler is ground fishing for other fish.

The turbot, after the halibut, is the largest flat fish on the British List and can run over 40 lb in weight. The upper side is brownish with dark blotches and there are a number of pimples on the top. Its shape is roughly that of a diamond. A big fish like this needs strong tackle and the hook should be a large one.

The *Brill* is another flat fish fairly plentiful round our coasts, which prefers to live in deep water and therefore is not often caught by the amateur. Its shape is more rounded than the turbot and it can weigh anything up to a stone. The upper side is greyish-brown covered with blotchy patterns.

The *Herring*, much to the surprise of many people, figures in the list of sporting British fishes. The herring is a good sporty fish and will take a small spinner. Trout tackle and trout-sized hooks with a white winged fly will also lure the herring. The best time for herring angling is from June to the end of December, in the evening, or in the twilight just before dawn.

The *Smelt* is the name given to two species of fish. The first, the true smelt, is also known as the sparling while the other is known as the atherine or sand smelt.

The true smelt is a delicate looking, silvery fish chiefly found off the Norfolk and Lincolnshire coasts and not found off the Southern coast. The atherine is, however, plentiful on the South and scarce on the East coast. The true smelt is a member of the salmon family and can be identified by having two back fins, the rear one having no rays and being fatty. The atherine, which also has two back fins, has perch-like spines on the small front fin, while the rear fin contains rays and is non-fatty. Both these species frequent harbours and estuaries and the true smelt spawns in fresh water. In Lincolnshire the true smelt is frequently caught in drains and docks. The season for fishing both fishes is from September to March.

Angling methods require very light tackle and this is where the true roach fisher comes into his own. Ground baiting is the key to success and the hook should be small. The true smelt also gives off a faint smell of cucumber when freshly caught and is a delicacy on the table, though the atherine is quite tasty eating also. Smelt are not large fish for they rarely run to more than about 7 in. in length.

The *Dogfishes* are sometimes welcome and sometimes heartily cursed by the angler. The professional hates them as they attack the fish he is after: the match angler welcomes them, sometimes, when trying to make a big bag (unless barred from the contest by special rule). The dogfishes are small sharks and they are greedy, fierce, and will take almost any bait. Once they are in the area they will drive all other fishes away. They are of little value as food, though, again, they appear under the heading of 'Rock salmon' in the fish-and-chip shops!

There are several species in British waters. There is the spur-dog, or picked dog, which carries in front of each back fin a sharp spike. As it can grow to a length of 3 ft and is a strong fish, it requires a bit of handling to be brought in.

The rough-hound, rowhound, or lesser spotted dogfish,

also runs to 3 or 4 ft length and its skin contains a substance which causes it to bleach any other fish with which it comes into contact after capture.

The most popular dogfish, from the angler's standpoint, is the bull huss, or large spotted dog, or nurse hound. This fish carries spots like a leopard and is specially sought by the keen angler. It can attain a length of 5 ft and this length and weight, coupled with its ferocity, makes it a tough customer to land.

The *Weever* is the most dangerous fish in British waters

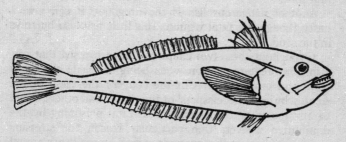

18 The most dangerous fish in British waters, the Lesser or Viper Weever. Note the spines on the dorsal fin and behind the gill covers which carry poison. The painful wound inflicted by this fish could be lethal

(Fig. 18). It is also known as the sting-fish and may be present in either of two species, the greater weever and the viper. The smaller of the two is the more dangerous.

Weevers should be dispatched when caught and handled with care both before and after the killing for they are equipped with sharp spines on the dorsal fin and behind the gill covers which pass a poisonous fluid into punctures caused in the flesh. THESE PUNCTURES CAN BE FATAL. Even in cases where the injured person is not very susceptible to shock, the resultant wound can be extremely painful. Weevers burrow into the sand leaving only their eyes exposed and therefore take the lures offered by the bottom fisherman. Bathers, paddling children, and others who walk barefooted into the sea run a grave risk of being hurt by this little fish. To assist in the identification of such a dangerous little monster, a sketch of one is given on the previous page (Fig. 18). It should be emphasized that even after the weever has been killed, the spines are still dangerous. To avoid risk of injury many professional shrimpers sort their catch with a piece of wood and very rarely enter the water except when wearing rubber boots. The spines can, it should be noted, pierce through the sole of ordinary plimsolls.

Another dangerous fish is the dragonet; it can give a nasty though not fatal wound. This little fish also burrows in the sand.

Throughout these two chapters I have stressed that certain fishes require caution when being handled: the sharp teeth and powerful jaws of the conger: the teeth of the small whiting: the 'claspers' of the skate: and others, down to and including the possibility of fatal poisoning by the diminutive weever. One particular reason for stressing caution is the fact that wounds caused by sea fishes are all liable to turn septic, even if only slight in the first instance, and they should be treated with an antiseptic immediately. It is sound practice to carry a small pocket first-aid kit, with a bottle of recognized antiseptic, in your gear when going sea angling.

Chapter 16

GROUND FISHING

GROUND FISHING is the term used by sea anglers to denote the type of fishing approximating to the coarse fisherman's 'bottom fishing.' The usual methods practised are (1) the sea leger and (2) the paternoster in one or other form.

The type of fishing determines the type of rod. For instance, where the angler is going to fish from a sloping beach and has to cast a considerable distance, say 100 yd or over, then he will require a long, powerful beachcasting rod. If, on the other hand, he is going to fish from a jetty or from a promontory, which does not entail a long cast, then a short rod would be better. For the beachcaster a length of 10 to 14 ft would be required, and here the physique and stature of the angler is of paramount importance. A short angler cannot handle a long rod as easily as a tall one. It needs a fairly tough physique to angle all day with very heavy equipment, handling a rod, say 12 ft in length, and casting weights of about 6 to 8 oz.

The whole question is complex, for the type of fish being sought, the stature of the angler, the nature of the terrain over which the angler will fish, plus the length of the angling day, have all to compromise and balance. If the tackle chosen is not correct, then there will probably be over-exertion, loss of efficiency, and a great many disappointments.

Bottom or ground fishing may also be carried out from a boat as well as from the shore. But for boat fishing a beachcasting rod would be ridiculous. A shorter rod is required, and, quite often, a rod suitable for boat work will also be found suitable for pier and jetty work.

Furthermore, during the course of a day's angling, the conditions will change several times. Owing to the tide, there are periods of no current, little current, strong tidal currents and eddies, followed by a series of reverse currents. In the space of a few hours the sea angler will experience all the conditions encountered by the freshwater loch fisher, plus the effects of a low river, a river in normal flow and a river in full spate!

This means, in effect, that to be successful the angler should change his tackle and/or methods to suit these hourly changing conditions.

In ground fishing the baited hook has to lie either on the sea bed, or fairly close to it. The simplest form of ground tackle to use is the sea leger.

Sea Leger

This consists of either a flat lead, or a bullet, with a hole bored through it, threaded to a piece of rustless wire about 18 in. in length. This piece of wire should have a loop at each end to which are attached swivels.

Below the lead and linked to the wire is a strong trace up to about 4 ft in length and to which the hook is attached. The upper end of the wire is attached to the line.

The principle of the sea leger is the same as in the freshwater leger. After the line has been cast the bait will lie on the bottom and when a fish takes the angler feels it at once as the wire is drawn through the lead.

A simple method to make a sea leger on the spot is to thread the weight on to the line and then nip a swan shot above and below the lead to prevent it slipping down on to the hook. But swivels should be incorporated into the rig as the action of the tidal currents causes the bait to swing about. When the line is recovered or when a fish takes there is a tendency of the line to twist and kink; swivels help to combat this.

The leger may be used from shore or from boat and it is not essential that it lie on the bottom when fishing from a pier or from a small craft. Sometimes the bait may be cast or lowered into the water and then drawn up so that it lies a few inches above the sea bed.

Paternoster (Fig. 19)

This may be used in several different forms and it is a very efficient method of ground fishing. The simplest form consists of a lead at the bottom of a trace and two or more hooks attached by simple loops. The disadvantage lies in the fact that the hooks often snag up and entwine themselves round the line. A better form of paternoster, shown in the accompanying sketch, incorporates booms from which the hooks are suspended but the best form is undoubtedly

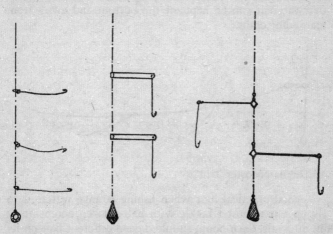

19 The sea paternoster. (*Left*) simple paternoster: (*centre*) plastic boom type: (*right*) straight pull boom

the 'straight pull' boom in which the hooks are spread to either side and less liable to catch up with each other on the line.

When fishing over a sandy bottom the lowest hook may be placed directly over the lead, but if fishing over a rocky or pebbly bottom the lowest hook should be placed at such a height above the lead that it will not catch on the bottom.

A variation of the paternoster is the *Paternoster Trot* (Fig. 20). This consists of a trace, bearing two or more hooks, attached to the line by means of a swivel. Some anglers are tempted to use half-a-dozen hooks with the paternoster trot, but this, in practice, is a delusion. Too many hooks means more time spent in baiting up, more bait used, and the chances of being snagged or caught up in underwater obstacles are increased. When using the paternoster trot it sometimes pays to add an extra boom and hook about 12 to 18 in. above the swivel. Quite often fish will take the bait on the higher hook while the lower hooks remain untouched. One advantage of the paternoster over the leger is that the bait can be kept off the bottom and away from marauding crabs.

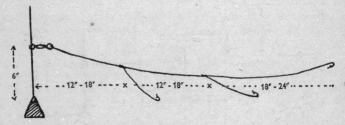

20 The paternoster 'trot'

A good practical hint when fishing strange waters is to rig up a paternoster tackle with half-a-dozen booms at 12 in. intervals. Each boom should have a different bait on its hook, so that the angler can ring the changes, as it were, and experiment until he finds the right bait at the right height for those special conditions. When he finds this he should then revert to a two hook paternoster and fish in the normal way, or change his tackle to suit the prevailing conditions.

Paternoster tackle is good for boat and pier fishing, but it can also be presented in another form, known as the spreader (Fig. 21). This consists of a boom from either end of which hooks are hung. The lead is attached to the centre of the boom and attached to the line by a swivel. This tackle works very well when lowered from pier or boat to the sea bed and gradually raised until it is found at what depth the fish are interested, and thereafter fishing at that depth.

Do not be put off by arguments advanced in articles in the angling press that brass paternoster booms spoil the fishing. The theory is that they shine and scare off the fish. In gin clear waters, and how rarely does one get these conditions, there may be some substance in this argument, but

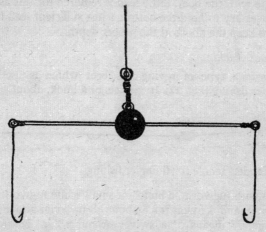

21 The 'spreader' for boat or pier fishing

under normal angling conditions, when the water is murky owing to tidal movements, or the day is dull, or the water fished is fairly deep, the flash of the paternoster boom, rather than acting as a deterrent, actually lures the fish to the bait. But if the angler has bought bright brass booms and now feels unsure to use them, he can take the shine off the brass by immersing them in vinegar.

In actual fact I often make my paternoster lures attractive. I wrap silver paper or cooking foil on the nylon or gut just above the hook, and sometimes at intervals along the line in an attempt to attract fish on to the lure. I have found that this works effectively when biting has been slow, and pollack and bass, for example, have taken when other, conventional anglers alongside me have had no bites at all.

Drift Paternostering

This is a method used by boat anglers. The normal paternoster rig is used and it is carried out over a sea bed which is clear of weeds. The paternoster tackle is lowered to the required depth and allowed to drift up and down in the tide with the boat. Little lead is required for this as it is not necessary to hold the bottom : just sufficient lead being used to keep the hooks at the proper depth.

'Wander' Tackle

This is a type of roving sea leger which is used for flounder fishing (Fig. 22). It consists of a hook, about size 4,

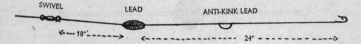

22 'Wander' tackle for flounder fishing

baited with lugworm, a bunch of small white ragworms, or soft crab, and a nylon trace about 48 in. long, attached to the line by means of a swivel. About 18 in. below the swivel a spiral lead about ½ to 1 oz weight is fixed, and between the spiral lead and the hook a small anti-kink lead.

The Wander tackle is used by casting and allowing it to sink to the bottom and then gradually recovering the line. The main lead stirs up the mud or sand on the bottom and this attracts feeding flounders which then go after the bait. The recovery rate is not like spinning, it must be very slow, and crabs can often be a nuisance. To beat crabs a small cork may be attached to the trace about 8 in. above the hook and the anti-kink lead dispensed with. This raises the baited hook from the sea bottom.

When using Wander tackle from the shore it is merely cast out and then methodically recovered. When using the tackle from a boat all it is necessary for the angler to do is lower the hooks over the side until the lead reaches the bottom, and then allow it to drift along with the boat!

Bottom Fishing for Tope

The equipment for tope fishing is similar to big game tackle. A stout fibre-glass rod is necessary and the large diameter reel should hold up to 300 yd of line with a breaking strain up to 40 lb. The hook should be large, at least 1 in. gape, and a pliable *steel* trace about 6 to 12 ft in length completes the tackle. The trace must be longer than the body of the tope, which can be 5 ft, because if the fish swims away from the angler one blow from its tail could

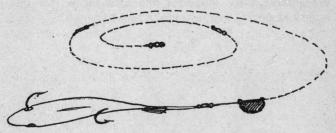

23 Tope tackle baited with a whole mackerel

sever the line; again piano wire is recommended for this trace which may have to withstand the attacks made upon it by the sharp teeth of this small shark.

The hook is baited with a whole herring or mackerel which is threaded on by a baiting needle. A second hook is usually used so that there is one hook through the head of the bait and another through the tail (see illustration Fig. 23). Above the baited hook is a sliding lead, about 8 ft above the wire trace. The tackle is fished as follows. The mounted bait is lowered into the water but immediately under the sliding lead an ordinary matchstick is attached to the line by a clove-hitch. This is to prevent the sliding lead from running on the trace. The lead is lowered to the sea bed and allowed to remain still. Some anglers like to raise the bait just clear of the sea bed.

The tope, in spite of its ferocious nature, takes the bait very gently and when hooked makes strong and sustained rushes in attempts to escape.

For fishes such as conger and skate, the running leger is found to be the best tackle to use: but for general fishing the paternoster can bring the angler a greater number of different species to his landing net.

Apart from flounder fishing, the bottom tackle should be fairly strong. In some coastal waters it may be necessary to use as much as 1 lb of lead to hold the bottom, tidal currents being so fierce.

Bottom fishing does not really come into the province of the enthusiast for ultra-light and light tackle. For that branch of angling we must turn to FLOAT FISHING.

Chapter 17

FLOAT FISHING

TO FISH on the bottom does not always spell success, for not all fishes seek their food there. Some are midwater feeders, others feed on or near to the surface. Again the raiding crabs may prove too much to cope with and the bottom angler has to either change his venue or change his rig.

Float tackle is used when it is necessary to keep a bait near the surface, or in midwater, though float tackle may also be used when the bait is fished on the bottom. In the first two cases the float serves the purpose of taking and carrying the bait to the fishes as well as acting as a signal when a fish has taken: but when the float is used with bottom tackle then its function is to act as a bite indicator only.

Float fishing is, in the main, confined to depths which are not much more than a rod length, i.e. in comparatively shallow water, or for keeping the bait near the surface. But float fishing may equally well be used from a boat as from the shore or pier.

Float fishing is divided into two classes, light and heavy. With light float tackle the angler will seek such fishes as the smelt, the mullet, and the mackerel. With heavy tackle he will seek the larger, more powerful fishes such as the pollack and the bass.

Sea floats are divided into two categories: fixed and sliding.

The fixed type of float is one which stays in position on the line: the sliding float (Fig. 24) is used for fishing in deep water and, as the name implies, is free to ride up and down the line.

The fixed float used chiefly is a pear-shaped cork bodied one. In the standard pattern there is a hole drilled vertically through the centre into which a removable hardwood plug is fitted. The line is threaded through the central hole, from which the plug is removed, and when it has been placed in its proper position on the line, the plug is replaced, holding it in position. By simply removing and replacing the plug as required, the float can be moved up and down the line to suit angling conditions.

24 A sliding float

An ordinary pike float makes a suitable one for this work.

The *Fishing Gazette* float is a variation on this theme. A slit is cut into the body of the float as far as the central hole. By removing the hardwood plug the line is easily inserted into or removed from the slit and this means that the float is easy to change without having to dismantle any of the tackle.

The sliding float (Fig. 24) has, usually, rings attached to its end and body centre through which the line may freely run. When the sliding float is placed on the line it immediately drops down to the lead. To use a sliding float the angler predetermines the depth at which the float is to work and at that point on the line attaches a piece of rubber tubing, thin enough to slip through the rod rings but sufficiently thick to prevent its being drawn through the float rings. When the tackle is used the float slides up the line owing to its natural buoyancy until it comes to rest against the rubber stop. When reeling in the angler can recover all his line as the float slips down the line towards the hook.

The sliding float is very important for deep water fishing, for if an ordinary float were used, attached to the line, and the angler had 18 ft between float and baited hook, the angler concerned would be in rather an invidious position trying to bring in a fish which had taken. He would have to resort to handlining the fish in because when the standard fixed float reached, and jammed, against his top ring he would be unable to wind in farther and the fish would still be in a fair depth of water.

The float tackle may be used in conjunction with paternoster rig and under suitable conditions of wind and tide, used without any lead, the weight of the baited hook being sufficient.

Surface Fishing

This is a specialist form of float fishing for mullet. This can only be used in conditions of calm or almost calm water and follows either of two forms: single hook surface tackle, or surface trot when two or more hooks are used (see illustrations, Fig. 25).

The tackle required is light. In the case of the single hook tackle the rig consists of a small cork float, or a small cork, a trace not more than 12 in. in length and hooks about size 8. The tackle is used by baiting the hook with bread paste, macaroni paste, or very small ragworms. Groundbait must also be used. The tackle is cast into the water a few yards

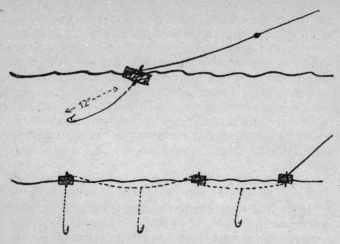

25 (a) Single hook surface tackle for mullet fishing.
(b) A surface 'trot' for mullet

upcurrent of where the mullet are cruising so that the water will carry it down to them.

When using the surface trot the principle is the same, but small cork floats are threaded on to the traces midway between the hooks.

Chapter 18

SPINNING AND WHIFFING

THE FRESHWATER angler will be a little nonplussed to find that the sea angler uses a variety of different terms to describe what he calls 'spinning'.

Whiffing is a familiar term. This corresponds to the normal straightforward freshwater spinning. This involves casting of the lure from the reel and recovering it.

Railing is another term. This is sometimes termed trolling. The method of fishing is not proper angling as it merely consists of towing a bait behind a moving boat. This is the method beloved of the novice holidaymaker angler who pays his two or three shillings for a trip round the bay so-called mackerel fishing.

Sometimes a trolling or railing lure is justified. When trying to find the area in which fish are feeding it sometimes pays the angler to put a railing bait over the side and then, when he takes a fish, to angle from that spot with conventional methods. Trolling or railing also helps to catch fish for bait on the way to the fishing spot.

Spinning techniques are basically the same as for freshwater angling and fixed-spool reels give excellent results. But whereas sometimes a straightforward recovery will bring freshwater fish after the lure, in salt water the best way to work a spinning lure is to use the 'sink and draw'. The reel handle is given a few quick turns, then the movement is stopped, and then repeated. When the line is recovered the bait is drawn through the water, but when the reel is stopped the bait commences to drop downwards towards the sea bed in a series of erratic movements.

If a heavy fish is taken the angler should try to 'pump' his fish. But one must not be careless when using this method, otherwise a rod may be ruined. The technique is simple.

The rod is merely brought from horizontal to vertical position using the suppleness of the rod against the fish. This must not be done quickly. When the rod is vertical or nearly so the tip is quickly dropped to the horizontal position and at the same time the loose line is recovered quickly on the reel. This means that, though only a few feet at a time are recovered, the angler is continually putting a steady strain on the fish, gradually recovering his line, and exhausting the quarry. Indeed with conger and skate pumping is probably the only sure way to success. But pumping must not be resorted to if a fish refuses to move. To try to pump under these circumstances means probably a broken trace, perhaps even a broken rod.

It is interesting at this point to digress and look into the origin of some of the sea angling terms. Railing was once called reeling and referred to the act of towing a baited fishing line behind a craft under sail. But if the craft was being rowed or sculled then the term used was whiffing.

Spinning for sea fish may be carried out from beach, from pier, as well as from boat. I like the side-casting Alvey reel for salt-water work, it is an uncomplicated piece of equipment, easy to clean and maintain, because salt water can play the very devil with metals. For light spinning work among school bass, mackerel, and flounders, I use an 8 ft fibre-glass spinning trout with a fixed-spool reel. For heavy spinning work, when I have had to cast considerable distances from a pier, I use a beachcaster and a fixed-spool reel or a side-caster. For boat work, I like to use the multiplier reel; it can be built much more substantially than either of the others, the Intrepid Sea-Streak being typical.

For ultra light work among the channels of estuaries I use what is termed a 'bait-casting' rod, with an offset handle, and a closed-face reel. This is light and suitable for the smaller sizes of fish encountered.

Using the light rod with fixed-spool reel, the technique is the same as for freshwater spinning. But, when using heavier tackle suited for the bigger species of sea fish, the continual casting and retrieving of heavy lines and lures plus a weight of $1\frac{1}{2}$ to 3 oz coupled with the drag and pull of a strong wind can tire even the toughest angler if the technique is not done correctly.

If using a multiplier reel, the little finger is used to apply pressure to the rim of the reel and act as a brake and the rod may be handled either with two hands, or for single-handed casting. For single-handed spinning the rod should be held in the right hand with the trace and lure hanging from the tip. The rod is then swung back, either straight overhead or to the side and then brought forward swiftly and smoothly. Then the rod is stopped short of the direction in which the cast is being made. The line will shoot forward and the spool of the reel will revolve. This is where the braking action of the finger (though some anglers prefer to use the thumb as a brake) comes into play, to prevent the spool from overrunning the speed of the line flow which creates backlash and ends up in a tangle of line commonly termed a 'bird's nest'.

In addition to spinning from pier, boat or beach, the angler can also do what is termed in America as 'surf casting'. This is a good sporting way of fishing. It entails the use of waders or hip boots for wading along the shore, or out to sandbars where one can cast into deeper water. Now with the conventional beach outfit the angler stands at the edge of the sea and makes long casts. Though long casting may be necessary in some areas, it is a fact that the long caster is often fishing *beyond* where the fish lie and this is where surf casting comes into its own.

For surf casting I would recommend a fibre-glass rod, about 6 to 7 ft in length. The rod must be sturdy yet flexible. But it is not necessary to cast fabulous distances for the successful surf angler will rarely cast more than 40 yd. When surf casting the angler searches the water area thoroughly with his lure. He is fishing within the shallows and at the same time reaching out and casting behind the breakers, where the big bass are wont to prey.

The mechanics of surf casting are as follows:

1. Place the reel fairly high on the butt of the rod then hold the rod directly under the reel with the right hand. Grasp the butt of the rod with the left hand, almost at the end.

2. Bring the rod tip back until the lure almost touches the ground or water behind you. When this is done the right hand acts as a pivot point but the left hand pushes the butt away from you.

3. Cast by pulling back on the butt with the left hand, at the same time pushing the upper part of the rod away with the right hand.

4. Follow through with the rod tip so that the line runs out straight.

5. When the lure hits the sea raise the rod to 45° and start re-winding. Vary the speed of recovery during the retrieve and work the lure at different depths.

Spinning Lures

These come in a great variety of shapes, sizes, and under a variety of names. They vary from a simple spinner to

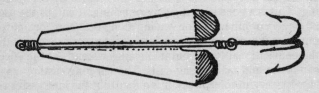

26 A mackerel spinner

elaborately dressed lures. The most popular type of spinner, certainly the cheapest to buy, is the Mackerel Spinner, consisting of an arrowhead shaped piece of metal with the rear portion bent into vanes (Fig. 26). This is mounted on to a flight containing a treble hook. They are usually silver or gold in colour, sometimes red and white or blue and white. There is also another spinner for mackerel known as the 'Dazzler.' This consists of three or more pairs of brightly coloured vanes mounted in front of a treble hook.

A popular lure is the rubber sand-eel (Fig. 27). One cannot beat the natural sand-eel as a bait, but some anglers prefer to use artificial lures, chiefly on the ground that they are not messy nor liable to become smelly.

27 The rubber sand-eel

The rubber sand-eel consists of a spinning vane with a swivel on to which is mounted a rubber tube. This rubber may be white, black, red, or green in colour. A large single hook is hidden in the body of the rubber-eel with point and barb protruding. This is a very good spinning lure for bass.

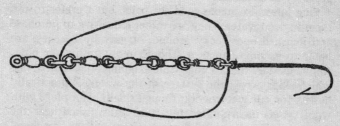

28 The baited spoon for flounder fishing

A deadly lure is the elongated spinner. This, usually made of polished metal and armed with a treble hook, may vary in size from $2\frac{1}{2}$ in. to 8 or 9 in.

Spoon baits, especially if a white wool tassel is fixed on to them, are very effective lures for bass, mackerel, coalfish, and pollack.

For flounders a special form of spinning, known as baited spoon angling, is used (Fig. 28). This consists of a spoon body attached by a spring link and swivel to the trace. From the spring link a series of swivels are linked together for the full length of the body of the spoon and terminate in a large single hook which stands well clear of the spoon itself. The hook is baited with ragworm, lugworm, or shell-fish and may be used to bring the flounder to basket. The spoon is often painted white, or sometimes white on one side and silver on the other. Baited spoon tactics may be used against other species than the flounder, of course.

In addition to spoons and similar lures, the angler may use dead natural bait, mounted to a spinning flight, and sprats are a first-class bait. Strips of oily fish mounted on single hooks, with a spinning vane in front, also make first-rate spinning lures.

Sea fish when on the feed will respond to even the simplest of spinning lures, especially when the angler is surf casting. If milk bottle tops or silver foil are placed on a bare hook and that is cast into the sea, if there are any predators about, such as bass or mackerel, the angler will probably be successful.

Plug lures also make good sea baits, but I prefer to use them in deep water. They are rather expensive to purchase and if fished over rocky ground, or gravelly beaches, are liable to become damaged. Though most freshwater plugs can be used by the sea angler the skipping plug, that is, one which skips across the surface of the water, is practically useless for salt water work, though small, plain plugs with wool tassels incorporated into their tails, fished near the surface, do bring a good response from pollack, mackerel and school bass.

Finally, one word of advice. The modern type of spinning reel, whether fixed spool or closed face, has a smooth clutch built into it. When properly adjusted this will slow the run of a fish without breaking the line. The drag can be varied at any time while playing a fish, but for sportiest fishing should be set lightly.

Whenever a fish runs the angler should stop winding in the fixed-spool reel. It is a novice's mistake to try to use the reel against the weight and strength of a fish when retriev-ing and the knowledge that the reel has a slipping-clutch mechanism is the angler's undoing. Every turn of the handle under these conditions places a twist in the line. Remember that the clutch, provided you handle the fish properly, will stop the line breaking and the correct use of the springlike action of the rod tip will wear the fish out. It has to be admitted that, within reason, light tackle will wear a fish out sooner than heavy tackle, though taking fish on light tackle means that a much longer time is taken. But there is a lot more fun in light tackle than in heavy tackle, as the angler soon finds out.

Chapter 19

FLY FISHING IN SALT WATER

THIS IS my own favourite method of salt water fishing. I do not claim that it is the best method, nor do I claim that it is the most skilful, for it is not. But aesthetically it is the most pleasant.

There is nothing new about fly fishing in salt water. It has been practised for about a century, but for a time it slipped into obscurity. However, today with present trends towards lighter and more sporting tackle for sea fishing, the fly fisherman has come into his own.

If the angler uses fly when seeking pollack or bass which are feeding near the surface, he will find that he is taking part in a sport which is every bit as good as salmon fishing, at a much lower cost. If he tries fly fishing against the mackerel, then he will find it on a par with sea trout angling. Again, subject to river authority licences, one can fish in the shallows of the coast for sea trout, with the fly. And excellent sport that is.

Fly fishing, as practised in salt water, is really not fly fishing at all. The lure represents a small fish or other aquatic creature and does not fulfil the conditions of 'fly' as demanded by the trout fishing purist. In fact, fly fishing in the sea rather approximates salmon fishing. The only link between fresh and salt water fly fishing lies in the fact that the lures are made from feathers, coupled with similar methods of casting.

Feathering, or the dragging of bunches or strings of white or coloured feathers or plastic dressed 'flies' through the water by commercial fishermen, is not and never has been 'fly fishing'. Feathering is a good method of taking mackerel and other surface feeding fish, but is often undertaken crudely, and the lures are generally railed.

A game fishing rod is required. The rod should be stiffish

in action and the reel should be large. Salmon fishing flies make first class, if expensive, lures and the rule is the brighter the fly the better it is for sea fishing. Mullet and mackerel will respond avidly to a sea-trout fly, but may be taken on the smaller trout flies under favourable conditions. For pollack a special fly is often used. This is termed a 'cuddy' fly and is generally dressed with white wings and a red woolly body on a large hook (Fig. 29). But for pollack a salmon rod is to be preferred to the light trout rod for the fish is a powerful fighter and when he takes the fly he does so in a vigorous manner.

Learning to cast the fly is the same as for the freshwater

29 A 'cuddy' fly

angler and the novice is referred to that chapter, but the sea angler should also learn to cast a fly with a two-handed rod.

Using a rod with the reel midway up the butt, one hand above and one below the reel, the rod is swung back over the shoulder by both hands. For a brief second its travelling is halted, then the tip is swished forward by pulling back the lower arm and pushing forward with the upper so that the upper arm is straightened. The rod is checked at about 45° to the perpendicular so that the line shoots forward.

Working the fly is best done from a boat but, of course, it may be practised from promontories and jetties. But a boat is the best platform for the factor of casting into, across or down the wind does not worry him. He can always cast downwind from a boat! Furthermore the use of a boat allows an angler to get near his fishes and this, again, means that as the casts are shorter in distance, they are better controlled, and this means, in turn, greater accuracy.

For obvious reasons fly fishing should not be carried on from a public pier: it can be a highly dangerous procedure for other anglers or spectators.

If the angler uses a cuddy fly, it should be worked more or less quickly across the surface but if the angler is using a salmon or sea-trout fly, then it should be worked in a series of jerks. These flies, too, should be worked well below the surface in order to take on the appearance of small fishes, and therefore attractive to the bass and other predatory fish.

It is difficult to know when to strike. The angler has no float to indicate to him that a fish is taking: he does not have the tight line of the leger: his attention has therefore to be given to the line itself. Do not watch the line where it enters the water, rather approximate the action of the man who is upstream working for trout. The line curves between rod tip and where it enters the water and it is this curve which must be watched. The moment it straightens is the moment to strike: striking being accomplished by merely tightening the line by raising the rod tip. A violent strike will lose a fish, either by tearing the hook away from his mouth, or tearing the mouth (in the case of mullet), or breaking the trace.

A sea fish is no tame taker of the fly! The moment a successful strike has been made the angler will be fully aware of the fighting fury on the hook. Keep the rod tip upright and keep pressure on the fish. A bass will use all his strength to run and smash the line: a pollack will dive determinedly to the sea floor: the mullet will make for the first underwater obstacle to take the line round: and the gallant mackerel will not yield in his effort to escape.

A rough day means that the fly should be large: if the day is bright the fly should be dark, whereas if the day is overcast or one is fishing at dusk, then the fly should be large and light. A fly with plenty of white or cream in the dressing, made from white hen feathers, is a good evening fly.

I have found that fished in the shallows of an estuary, where the water was little over a foot deep, a white cuddy fly was attractive to flounders, fished slowly along the bottom. Perhaps this may be regarded more as spinning than fly fishing, but at Bonddhu I took half a dozen flatfish with the cuddy when they would look at nothing else!

I would not advise the use of a trout fly line for sea angling. A good cuttyhunk line, with a breaking strain of 10 lb, makes a good line for this purpose. The freshwater fly line is easily damaged by the action of the salt water, and a nylon line is completely unsuitable on account of its stretching properties as well as being too light in weight. The flies, too, should be washed out in fresh water after use, otherwise they will corrode the hook, and the hook points should be kept absolutely sharp and touched up with a stone periodically.

Chapter 20

GENERAL HINTS

SO FAR we have considered the sea fishes likely to be caught, different methods of fishing, and tried to give a general picture of sea angling. However, before going on to the very big question of baits, the angler should be prepared to spend a little time studying the coastline or the waters where he is hoping to fish.

It is useless deciding to go sea fishing and then go straight off to the nearest coastline and hope to start catching sea fish at once! Some anglers do it, occasionally they are fortunate and bring fish home, but in the main it is a rather stupid way of going about it.

The angler, on visiting the coast for the first time, has to take note of several important factors and to do so means spending a considerable time on reconnaissance. First of all he has to note the nature of the shore, whether it is rocky, sandy, pebbly, boulder-strewn, and so forth. He must then note whether the shore shelves steeply, or runs out in shallows for a considerable distance. Do any rivers, streams, or sewers discharge into the sea near that point? Is there, for example, a power station on the coast which uses the sea water for cooling purposes or which discharges warm water into the sea? Are the beaches private and walking over them thereby constituting a trespass? These are the sort of questions which the angler must answer.

It behoves him, therefore, to walk along the shore and explore it fully. It may be necessary to walk along the base of cliffs, to see what escape routes there are back to safety if, fishing from rocks, the tide should be higher or earlier than anticipated. Only the stupid angler allows himself to be cut off by the tide, and this stupidity is downright selfish because it means other people have to be inconvenienced, perhaps even risk their own lives, to save the idiot who puts himself in such jeopardy.

He must walk the beach, explore the rock pools, note where patches of weeds are. He must watch the sea birds and observe if they congregate in bunches on the water, a sure sign of fish in the area. The height to which the tide runs up the beach, and a thorough exploration of the area it covers and uncovers, is important.

Storms cause the beach to change contour, channels appear and disappear, sandbanks and spits rise and are washed away, and all these things affect the angler.

He must study the shore and observe whether there are signs of, for example, shell-fish in the sand, mussels or limpet on the rocks, casts from sea worms exposed behind the tide.

Finally, and this does make the list seem formidable, he must study the tides thoroughly, the height to which they run and the times they ebb and flow: he must observe if there is a stand of the tide at low or high water: he must beware of the phenomenon of the double tide. The phases of the moon, which have effects upon tides, and an examination of a coastal chart of the water, form part of his curriculum.

Let us deal, first of all, with the tides. In the British Isles, for tides vary throughout the world, we have two types of tide, Spring Tides and Neap Tides. It is during the spring tides that the water movement is greatest, when tides are highest and retreat farthest. Half moon and full moon are times of spring tides. In first and third quarter of the moon, the lower, neap tides take place. Thus, spring tides have nothing to do with the season of that time. In March and September, there are what are termed Bird Tides, when the spring floods are reaching their highest marks.

But tides, though they may be predicted by special tables as to time and height, by such authorities as the Admiralty, cannot be predicted *exactly*. The time of the high water, or low water, may vary by anything up to an hour for meteorological conditions, high winds, excessive rains causing flooded rivers to build up against a making tide in an estuary, have their effects and cannot be predicted.

It follows, therefore, that predicted tide times and heights are, at best, an indication as to what the angler may expect to encounter.

Coupled with the tides are the effects of erosion on the coast. When the sea eats away portions of the coast, or does the opposite as by building up a gravel bank, the changes affect the fishes in that locality. And it is a sad fact that the best angling is usually enjoyed wherever there is erosion.

How then does the sea angler find his fish? Well, the first thing to do is watch the local anglers. Don't expect them to tell you exactly where to go and what bait to use: because, unfortunately, they are not likely to be very cooperative, and who is to blame them? I remember an instance, fishing on Bournemouth pier. I was fishing for mackerel with light float tackle, at a depth of 4 ft. Before setting up the tackle I had watched, from the top deck of the pier, as a spectator, two local anglers setting up this particular rig and bringing mackerel in. Within a few minutes I had landed a mackerel. I rebaited the hook and cast out and that was when one of the locals noticed me. 'Hello,' he said, 'just started?' I nodded. 'What you after?'

'Mackerel.'

'Well, I see you've got float tackle. Won't do no good, mister, they only take spinners. What depth you at?'

I told him.

'No good,' said he, without batting an eyelid. 'They're way down, 'bout eight feet. I 'spose you're using worm?'

'No, sprats.'

'No good. Rag, that's what you want.'

At that precise moment in the conversation another mackerel took my bait. My companion said nothing as I landed the fish. Two mackerel later, one to me and one to the local, he grinned and said, 'You've been here before.' And that was that.

No, watch what the local anglers do and where they fish. But don't, for heaven's sake, follow blindly, for the pier may be crowded with competition anglers, plus holiday anglers, and it may be the worst possible place to angle from.

Low water is the best time to try and find out about the fish. If the tide has underscored rocks, or scoured out a basin in the sand, these are the places worth dropping your bait in at high water. Floating weed often has fish round it, and sewage outfalls generally are good places for the fish hunter.

The time of the year is also important:

Bass, for example, are best in summer and autumn.
Cod are best during the winter months,
Whiting may be fished for during summer, autumn, and winter, but
Wrasse are summer fish only.

Most coasts can provide a bit of virgin territory to angle from, but the pier and jetty are different propositions. One is usually crowded for space and the rule is, first come first served. If fishing from piers and jetties, do not cut up bait on the boards, rails, or seats, for this is a messy and anti-social habit. Activities such as this get angling stopped in many quarters. Care must also be exercised when casting, and the angler must play any hooked fish carefully so as not to entangle other anglers' lines.

Knowledge of when to fish on the bottom or midwater is bought by experience, but a general rule is that at high water, and also when the tide is turning, the fish feed higher in the water. The evening, the very early morning, and the hour before and up to high tide are usually the best times: but I have had excellent days on the ebb, and also found that the first thirty minutes when the tide begins to flow are often the most productive in an angling day.

When it comes to going afloat the novice is best advised to employ a local boatman or professional fisherman who specializes in this work. The local tides, the nature of the sea bed, the presence of rocks, dangerous shoals, and effects of wind are known to the professional, and in the case of, say, fog, the novice would be needlessly risking his own life, perhaps the lives of others too, to go venturing on to the sea alone.

If hiring a boat, however, it pays to make certain that the craft is in good condition, that there is a baler available in case water is shipped, that the anchor rope is not frayed or rotten, and that the oars and rowlocks, or pins, are also in good condition.

Beware of the offshore wind.

This is a dangerous phenomenon and all too often the beginner finds himself miles offshore and unable to row back against a powerful tide and the wind.

Finally, no angler should go afloat unless he can swim and has got a life jacket or buoyancy belt with him.

On conclusion of the angling day the sea angler must carefully go over his tackle. The last few feet of the line must be examined for fraying where it has been pulled over gravel or round rocks or pier stanchions. All worn line must be discarded. The hooks must be examined for blunt points, traces examined for pulled eyes, and the lures cleaned in fresh water. The line must be washed out and dried and the reel, and rod fittings, cleaned and given a light touch of oil.

Under no circumstances throw nylon line or casts away into the sea or drop it on the beach. Nylon is apt to entangle in the legs of birds and cause them terrible suffering. Hooks, though they rust away in time, may pierce the foot of some bather, or hand of some child playing in the sand. Discard your old tackle in the correct way, into the litter bin or basket, or better by far, take it home for disposal.

If you have carried fish in a creel or bag, wash it out and dry it, hanging it up so that it can get thoroughly aired and get rid of the fishy odour.

Check the rod for loose rings or ferrules, and in particular check that there is no salt or sand inside the female ferrule. I also recommend that reel mechanisms be washed out with either methylated spirits or petrol before examination and cleaning. This helps to get rid of grit and dirt which is apt to get into it. If you find that any part is showing wear, then take it to the shop or agency dealing with that reel and get a replacement fitted. Otherwise it may let you down when you are into the fish of a lifetime.

Finally, never lift a fish into the boat, or up the pier, with your rod. Use a net or gaff or tailer for landing the fish : but only use your rod for casting, retrieving the lure, hooking, and playing the fish!

Chapter 21

BAITS

IN THE question of baits the sea angler scores heavily over the freshwater enthusiast for there is almost a super-abundance of baits available, both natural and artificial. The sea angler who confesses that he cannot fish because he has not got any bait is showing his lack of knowledge, or displaying an excessive amount of laziness and lack of comprehension.

Generally, sea baits are divided into two main classes, natural baits and artificial baits. Some artificial baits are constructed from natural material, e.g. soleskin fly, and should really be considered as natural baits.

Artificial baits have been dealt with in the chapters dealing with fly fishing and spinning.

Of natural baits, the angler should realize that most fish are predatory, and like to feed on their own species as well as other small fish and aquatic creatures. Sea worms, crustacea, and food washed into the sea via rivers and sewers, as well as thrown overboard from ships, all form part of the sea fish diet. Though most of the natural baits are obtained from the sea shore, such as lug worm, or from the sea itself, such as small fish, many can be obtained from the fishmonger's, from one's own kitchen (as for example bacon skin), or bought ready preserved from the tackle dealer.

Chief on the list of natural baits are fish baits. These should be purchased fresh (if not caught by oneself) and in that order the angler should choose, herring, garfish, pilchards, mackerel, sprats, eels.

For large fish, such as tope and conger, a whole or perhaps a half fish will be used, but for bass and mackerel it will be found sufficient, except when using sprats, to make several baits from one fish.

Before cutting up fish into bait the angler should be in possession of (*a*) a bait board, (*b*) a bait box, and (*c*) a thin, long-bladed, cork-handled knife.

The bait board is essential because otherwise it is not possible to prepare the baits properly. If one is fishing from a sandy or pebbly beach it will soon be realized how difficult, if not impossible, it would be to try and slice up a fish for bait without a hard base on which to work.

The use of a pier rail or seat, or a boat thwart, is unsatisfactory and anti-social, and can result in soiled or damaged clothing for some third party, as well as being unsightly. The bait box, which should be wooden, should have a hinged lid and must be kept scrupulously clean.

The following is the best method to adopt when cutting up a fish bait :

1. Remove the scales by scraping.
2. Lay the fish flat on the bait board and commencing at the tail cut along the backbone to the head.
3. Insert the knife under the backbone and remove it from the flesh.
4. Place one half of the fish skin side downwards on to the board and cut into diagonal pieces (see illustration,

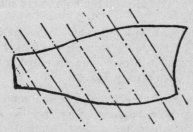

30 How to cut a fish into baiting strips

Fig. 30) each about 1 in. in width. The average mackerel will give about 8 or 9 such strips from each side.
5. To make a fish 'lask' or 'last', make a semi-circular incision into the fish about 2 in. from the tail and slice towards the tail. This removes a triangular piece of skin

(see illustration, Fig. 31) which should then have all the flesh scraped off it.

DO NOT THROW AWAY THE HEAD, BACKBONE OR ENTRAILS, ETC., OF THE CUT UP FISH. These should be collected into a

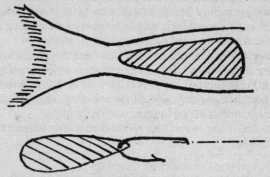

31 Preparation of mackerel or other fish 'lask' or 'last' and method of mounting on hook

bag and later used in the form of a ground bait or rubby-dubby.

Small fish, such as sprats, may be split down the middle, boned, and one side used on the hook. Very small fish may be used whole.

To bait the hook with fish strip – enter the point of the hook through the fleshy side of the darker portion of the strip, bringing it through, and then hook it through the lighter colour (see drawing, Fig. 32).

Remember that the bait must be in proportion to the hook. A large hook requires a large portion of bait, and vice versa. Of fish to use as bait – immature flounders, about $1\frac{1}{2}$ in. across, may be used, but only where absolutely necessary. They should be used whole.

Garfish is an excellent bait, as also is the gurnard and the mackerel. The sand-eel is a very popular bait, though in some localities I have known the rubber sand-eel taken when the fish have refused to look at the natural bait!

The sand-eel is best used as a live-bait with the hook point inserted into the mouth of the fish and out through the gills, or through the nape of the neck. For dead bait fishing the sand-eel should be mounted on single hooks, inserted through the mouth and emerging one third back from the head, or on two hooks with the lower hook inserted as in the case of a single and the upper hook through both lips.

From the kitchen one can obtain the common-or-garden kipper. This makes a first class bait and the kipper skin can be used for whiffing.

Most fish baits can be regarded as 'certainties', in so far as there are certainties in angling other than that the water is wet.

32 Method of attaching fish strip bait to hook

The next category of natural bait is the shell-fish. These are never to be regarded as 'killing' baits, for they are often refused by fish, but they are good standby baits. Shell-fish are easy to collect and sometimes do result in a fish taking which has refused all other baits. The chief disadvantage about shell-fish is the fact that they are not easy to place on a hook.

The cockle is common enough and though codling, pout, and flat fish will take it, it is not a very satisfactory bait. But, of course, better than none.

The limpet may be a first class bait on occasions, while at other times it is worse than useless. Limpets present a problem to the novice as they refuse to be collected unless the angler has the know-how. Once they are touched they resolutely stick to the rocks and are virtually impossible to move : but, if they are tapped on the side of the shell with a small hammer, or back edge of a knife, they are picked off quite easily.

For use as a bait the limpet must be removed from the shell whereupon it will be found that the fish consists of two portions, one hard and one soft. The hook point is introduced through the soft portion and then pressed through the hard one. Some anglers complete the job by tying soft wool round the bait and hook shank to keep the bait on the hook, but this is not necessary.

Mussels are probably the best of the shell-fish baits and are easily collected from groynes, pier stanchions and so on. Cod like mussel, preferably those collected from estuarial waters. And, a good hint if dogfish are in the area and the angler wishes to avoid them, these small sharks will not look at a hook baited with mussels.

Opening mussels presents its own problem. First of all examine a mussel and it will be seen that it is straight on one side and curved on the other. Hold the mussel with the narrow pointed edge in the palm and gently push the upper shell sideways, then into the tiny opening made insert the point of a knife. Pass the blade between the body of the mussel and the lower half of the shell and cut the fish's attachment away from the shell. This is done by cutting along one side of the powerful muscle which holds the two shells together. The mussel itself must remain unbroken in the shell half.

A second problem is now posed. How does one place this soft mass on the hook and keep it there? The hook should be pressed through the mussel from side to side and the point pressed into the white muscle which had to be cut before the shell was opened. If done properly the bait should stay on the hook without the necessity of any thread or wool to secure it.

The whelk is another good shell-fish bait, and the winkle can be used at a pinch, but the best shell-fish bait is the solen or razor fish. These are found buried in the sand and are very rapid movers. Sometimes they may be found with a portion of the shell sticking out of the sand and a quick, firm pull should result in a gathered razor fish. They are either dug for with a narrow spade or extracted with the aid of a small spear-like hook which is thrust down the blow-hole where the fish is.

Sea worms stand high on the list of first class baits. King ragworms, lugworms, will be found advertised in the angling papers, can be ordered by post and will be dispatched per passenger train with carriage extra. The sea worm digging industry must be quite large and hundreds of thousands of sea worms sold weekly. But the sea worm is rather an expensive bait and in many cases the cost of the bait exceeds that of hooks and terminal tackle! Assuming that an angler orders and receives his sea worms in good time, he must allow for a certain percentage of casualties before he can use them, and this all adds to the cost. But, though I like to hunt for and dig my own bait, the inexperienced angler who starts out on a bait-digging excursion to obtain a sufficient number of worms for a day's fishing will find that purchasing them is not all that expensive after all! In the beginning the novice will dig plenty of holes, and get an aching back, but by tackling the job right he will find ultimately that sea worm collecting is nothing like the arduous job it is made out to be in some quarters.

Lugworms live in the sand. They eat their way through it and after extracting what nourishment they can, pass it through their bodies. The sand which passes through the worm is thrown up on the surface of the sand in the form of a coil, and is known as a cast. About 12 to 18 in. from the cast there will be found a blow-hole and the lugworm lies midway between these two points in a U-shaped tunnel (Fig. 33).

The angler has to dig methodically, but once he has started digging he must be quick because the worm can burrow like lightning. Using a three-tined fork, or a very narrow spade, the angler should stand astride the cast and blow-hole. The implement should be eased into the sand about 6 in. in front of the blow-hole and a spit removed. The worm should now be in the channel behind the fork.

The angler follows up by digging a channel the width of the fork in steps towards the cast. As soon as the track or channel of the worm is found the fork or spade should be inserted quickly behind the worm which is then lifted clear of the hole. He must be careful not to damage the worm because in that case it becomes useless as a bait and also has the unpleasant habit of exuding a nasty reddish-yellow fluid which stains the fingers.

Lugworms can be kept alive for a few days in a wooden box of wet sand or seaweed, stored in a cool place. Dead and sickly worms must be removed promptly.

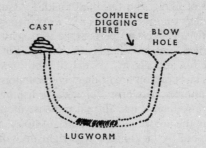

33 Showing how lugworms lie in their holes and where to commence digging

The lugworm makes a good leger bait, and is a very good bait to use with the baited spoon for flounder fishing. To attach a lug to the hook, the point should be inserted through the head of the worm and brought out about one third of the way down the body.

Ragworms lie in the mud and do not make a cast. They do not lie as deep in the mud as the lugworm, but they do make a vent hole which betrays their whereabouts. They may be dug for in a similar manner to lugworms. The ragworm looks like a cross between a centipede and a worm because it has a pair of feet attached to each body segment. It is a rather beautifully coloured creature, but the head contains a pair of pincers which can deliver a nasty, blood-drawing nip to the careless handler.

Ragworm may also be found lying under stones and in the cracks of rocks, and sometimes behind a hermit crab in the tip of a whelk-shell. Small white ragworms are to be found in the ooze in harbours and estuaries and these are popular with the mullet.

Earthworms may be used as estuary bait, and flounders and eels will take them in brackish water. They are not much use, however, in salt water, though it is unsafe to be dogmatic about anything pertaining to sea angling!

Crustacea

Though the sea angler will curse the hungry crab which contrives to rob his baited hook, none the less crab used as a bait earns the blessing of most sea anglers. Indeed, crustacea are fairly easy to obtain, clean to handle, and most fishes prefer them to other baits.

Crabs. The ordinary green crab which may be found in almost every pool, or under the larger stones on a pebbly

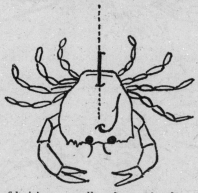

34 Method of baiting a small crab on a hook

beach, is a very good bait, but it should not be used more than about a halfpenny in size. The small green crab is baited whole on the hook as shown in the drawing (Fig. 34). However, the green crab is an obliging chap, for though it may be used whole if small, as it grows out of its shell, several times yearly, it casts the armour of the shell and goes and hides in any nook or cranny it can find until the new shell grows hard. During this period it is known as soft crab, and a very attractive bait it is too. If of any size at all they must be cut up into pieces to place on the hook. Larger crabs, even those with hard shells, can be killed and crushed up and mixed with other portions of fish, etc., and used as a ground bait.

Hermit crab. This is a very good bait but not always easily obtained. The tail of a hermit is a particularly attractive bait for whiting and flat fish.

Shrimps and prawns. These may be used either as a live or dead bait and are attractive for mullet, flat-fish, bass, pollack, eels, and, if placed on the hook in a small size about as big as a pea, smelts.

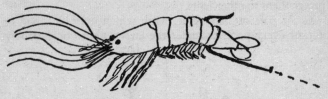

35 How to mount live shrimp or prawn on hook

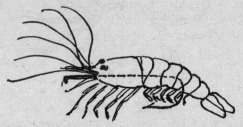

36 Mounting of dead prawn or shrimp bait.

If prawns or shrimps are used as a live bait, they should be hooked through the tail : if as a dead bait then they should first be boiled and mounted on a spinning flight. Methods of mounting live and dead prawns and shrimps are shown in the accompanying drawings (Figs. 35 and 36).

Other baits

Squid and octopi are first-class baits, except for one thing. They are apt to go 'high' very quickly and are only at their best when used fresh. Though octopus is a good bait, it is not very abundant on the English coast and the squid is more often used. The body, which is semi-transparent green, is cylindrical-shaped. Much more common, and also a very good bait, is the cuttle-fish. This may be seen floating in thousands upon the surface of the sea, especially in the Solent. This has very tough flesh. Though the flesh is itself a good bait, the tentacles as well as strips of the skin are also excellent baits. Conger are partial to fresh squid and cuttle, and the latter makes a good whiffing bait for bass, pollack, and coalfish.

From the kitchen, or from the butcher's, the angler will find a whole series of baits! These include tripe, bacon skin, and macaroni! Tripe, cut into long thin strips can be used as a whiffing bait for pollack, bass, and mackerel. The bacon skin should be scraped and cut into long strips about 3 in. in length and $\frac{1}{2}$ in. wide. Mounted on to a large hook and bound securely above the shank with thread it should be used like the rubber sand-eel. Predatory fish usually take bacon skin presented in this way avidly. Bacon skin, scraped clear of all flesh and fat, can be used in the manner of a fish 'lask', and is often used to make an imitation cuttle-fish.

Macaroni is a very good bait for grey mullet fishing. It should be boiled first, though I have made a good paste from it by merely soaking it until soft. Used for mullet it should be placed round a size 7 hook so that the whole hook, including the point, is covered. A generous ground-baiting of chopped boiled macaroni is necessary when this bait is used.

Groundbaiting

For many years groundbait was regarded as the mark of the coarse fisherman. Today there is an increasing realization that for successful sea-angling groundbaiting is often an essential operation.

But common sense must be used. For example, it is absolutely useless baiting up a fishing position if eddies and currents are going to take the groundbait far afield. Again, it would be stupid to groundbait an area, with a view to fishing it later, in a well-populated spot where other anglers could observe the preparations, and move in when the groundbaiting had been completed! The first purpose of groundbaiting is to give the fish a taste for the particular bait which you are going to introduce to them. The second purpose of the groundbait is to keep the fish in that area.

It is better to use too little rather than too much groundbait. And the tide times and flows are important when groundbaiting is taking place.

For example, portions of fish, crabs, and so forth, mixed up and dropped into the sea at slack water will remain in that area during the tidal stand. The angler can then fish throughout that period. But, if the tidal currents are running then the groundbait must be placed in such a position upcurrent that it will travel with the tide, gradually dropping towards the sea bed, until it is in the area of the baited hook. It follows, too, that for fast currents heavier portions of groundbait are required than in slack water.

If fishing in fairly deep water the groundbait should be sunk to the bottom. This may be done by filling a brown paper bag with bait, putting a stone inside, fastening the neck with string and lowering it to the bottom. When it is desired to release the groundbait the string is given a sharp jerk and the bag will burst, strewing the groundbait in the fishing area.

Portions of oily fish, such as herring or pilchard, can be put inside an old nylon stocking, some pebbles added, and the baited stocking dropped overboard. The globules of oil will travel downstream bringing the hungry fish upstream to the groundbait, and the baited hook. The shark angler uses a similiar method when dropping his 'rubby-dubby' sack overboard.

When fishing from a boat, if fish are taking on or near to the surface the groundbait may simply be cast overboard. If fishing from rocks it is a sound practice to spread groundbait along the rocks just above the tide line. The advancing tide sweeps the groundbait into the sea and to the fish in that area, keeping them in that spot and on the feed.

The wise angler will preserve some natural bait for future use. There is nothing difficult about it, all that is required are glass preserving jars and a formalin solution. This consists of 2 per cent formalin, 5 per cent glycerine, and 93 per cent *distilled* water. The small fish are merely washed and placed in a screw-top preserving jar containing that solution. Before use the bait should be washed and then put in a cloth impregnated with pilchard oil and then used normally.

Fish strip may be washed and then placed in a saturated solution of salt, which is made simply by adding salt to water until no more will dissolve. Shell-fish, which should first be removed from the shell, and shrimps and prawns may be preserved in a saturated salt solution. Whatever method is used, however, the containers must be air-tight.

Sand-eels may be preserved by placing them in a jar containing a mixture of equal parts of water, glycerine, and methylated spirits. After about a fortnight the jars should be examined and the mixture changed. A further change should be made about 14 days later to remove all oils given off by the dead fish. Before using, it is advisable to rinse off all preserved baits in water and a good tip is to smear them with pilchard oil immediately before using.

Part IV

General

Chapter 22

MAKE DO AND MEND

THIS CHAPTER applies to all branches of angling.

During the close season there is no need for the fisherman to sit twiddling his thumbs, bemoaning the fact that he is unable to follow his sport. The close season is the period when he can get down, seriously, to the task of examining, overhauling, and repairing his tackle and, with a little practice, the making of lures and other items of equipment.

The Rod

Repair and renovation of rods need present no especial difficulty. Many rods suffer damage during transportation, while the dropping of them may result in damaged rings and guides. A lined ring may become chipped and this, in

37 Snake type of rod ring

turn, means the possibility of frayed line. The worst casualties in this respect are those rods which use porcelain-lined rings. Snake rings often stand a lot of abuse, however (see Figs. 37 and 38). It is a simple matter to prevent this damage by plugging a porcelain-lined ring with a cork, which should be a tight fit.

The fitting of new rings to a rod is not a difficult job at all. But the new rings must be placed in the exact position occupied by the old ones. Should rod rings or runners show signs of rust they should be removed from the rod. This is done by cutting the whipping lying directly on the ring, not on the rod, by a razor blade, and then peeling it away. To refit rings, place them in the proper position by securing one foot of the ring with Scotch tape, This overcomes the problem of trying to hold the ring in position with one hand and attempting to put on the binding with the other.

Binding is done by putting a few turns of the whipping silk neatly, pressing it together and pulling it tight. The whipping may be wound round the rod, or the binding may be attached to one end of a frame and the rod, held horizontally, revolved so that each turn of the binding is

38 Bridge type of rod ring, with porcelain liner

put on evenly. The greatest problem arises in finishing off the whipping. This may be done by one of three ways:

1. Insert a piece of strong thread, doubled into a loop, into a couple of turns of the whipping, with the loop towards the end to be finished. Slip the loose end of the whipping through the loop and then withdraw the looped thread so that the end of the binding material is tucked under the whipping, or

2. Make the last few turns of the whipping over a matchstick. This means that the end of the whipping may be passed through the small gap thus formed. The matchstick is withdrawn, the lashing pulled tight and the loose ends cut flush, or

3. A bodkin or large needle may be used in lieu of the looped thread method in 1.

After one end of the whipping has been completed, the

temporary binding of Scotch tape can be removed and the binding at the other end finished off.

Rods, other than fibre-glass rods, may be damaged by taking a permanent 'set' or warping. This may be due to leaning the rod against a wall, or through excessive strain when playing a fish, or trying to recover a snagged-up lure.

A pronounced bend may be cured by removing the rod rings and replacing them on the opposite side of the rod. This is rather unsightly and does interfere with casting, but in time will put the rod straight.

A varnished rod is liable to suffer scratches and chips in its surface. This lets moisture in and can ruin the rod in next to no time. The scratches can be temporarily repaired at the waterside by a dab of nail varnish (all anglers should keep a small bottle of this in their kit for emergency use). But the only cure is to remove the old varnish completely with a light coat of varnish remover, then rub the surface down with very fine glasspaper. The new varnish should be evenly applied and a *matt* finish obtained. A nice, new shiny rod may look pleasant but the flash from a high varnished rod is one thing which is absolutely guaranteed to scare fish off quicker than anything else.

Rods should not be left lying about a room or leant againt a wall. They should be put in their covers and suspended from hooks so that they are not in contact with each other or with a wall. A good method is to suspend the rod from a hook screwed into the underside of a shelf. In angling warehouses rods are laid on each other in great piles: but as they are only there for a few hours no harm is done to them.

Simple spinning lures are easily made at home. Here are two which the angler can make for himself.

Flat Tube Minnow

This is made from a piece of copper or brass tubing. A piece of about 2 in. in length is suitable for freshwater fishing, and up to 4 in. for sea angling. The copper tube should be heated in the flame of a gas stove until it becomes red hot then immediately dropped into cold water. The angler should then make up a piece of brass wire slightly longer than the cut tube and make a loop at each end (see illustration, Fig. 39). This is placed into the tube which is then hammered flat, or placed in a vice and squeezed flat. The flattened tube containing the wire is then twisted. The amount of twist decides the rate of spin when the lure is drawn through the water. When this has been done the lure should have a swivel attached to one loop, and a treble

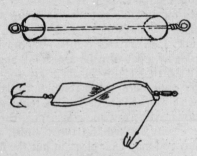

39 A home-made spinning lure from copper tubing. (*Top*) Showing wire mount inserted in tube prior to latter being flattened. (*Bottom*) Complete lure

hook attached by another swivel at the opposite end. Apart from touching up with a file, and perhaps a little paint, the lure is now ready for use.

Rubber Sand-eels

This consists of a piece of gas tubing about 6 in. in length. The tubing should be cut to a taper about one-third along its length. The mount is made from a piece of rustless wire and this is bent into a sharp curve. A treble hook is attached to one end, the other being bent into a loop. The complete mount is then threaded through the tubing from the tail, with the treble protruding from the base of the taper. The rubber tube is then secured below the mount by binding, and a swivel attached to the head loop.

Around him the angler will see plenty of materials which can be pressed into service as lures. Old toothbrush handles heated and twisted make first-class spinners! He may find that empty detergent containers make good sea floats, while ball-point pen reservoirs come in useful for many purposes.

Knots

Avoiding the obvious puns, this is a complex subject. There are only a few basic knots which the angler must learn to tie, and I feel that these are best learnt through the medium of illustrations rather than the written word, and the beginner should practise with some thick cord to start with. Knots should become easy to tie: tying of them should be done automatically by the angler so that he can tie a knot merely by the *feel* of the line or trace, without having to look at them.

It must be remembered that whenever a knot is tied in a line of trace, then it weakens the trace or line accordingly. Some knots weaken the material more than others. The angler should practise tying the following knots.

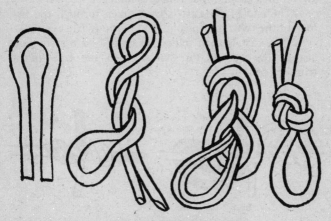

40 Stages in the tying of the Blood Bight Knot

Blood bight (Fig. 40).

1. Take the cast and bend it back on itself to form a loop (A).
2. Now twist this loop round the cast until it forms another loop (B).
3. Loop (A) is then passed through loop (B).
4. The knot is pulled tight and the free end cut off.

41 The Half Blood Knot

Four-turn half blood (Fig. 41). This is used to attach a cast or line to a swivel.

1. The end of the cast is taken through the eye in the swivel then wound four times round itself.
2. The end of the cast is then taken through the first loop of the twist, i.e. the one next to the swivel eye.
3. The cast is then pulled up tightly so that it binds against the eye of the swivel, then the free end is trimmed off.

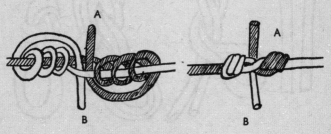

42 The Double Three-fold Blood Knot

Double three-fold blood (Fig. 42). This is for joining two casts together, or two portions of line of equal thickness.

1. Place the two ends alongside each other then twist the end of one three times round the shaft of the other.
2. Pass the end of this twisted cast through the space formed where the ends cross.
3. Now twist the end of the other shaft three times round the first one and pass the free end through the opposite space, as in 2 above.
4. Pull the knot tight and cut the loose ends off.
5. If, however, one wishes to attach a dropper to the cast, one of the loose ends may be left uncut.

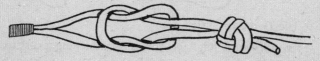

43 How to attach two loops

Two-loop knot (Fig. 43). For use where a loop is whipped on to the end of a line.

1. Pass the line loop through a loop in the cast, then thread the cast through the line loop.
2. Pull on the line and cast until the knot is tight.

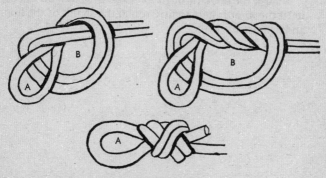

44 The Double Overhand Loop Knot

Double overhand loop (Fig. 44).

1. Bend the cast until a loop is formed, then twist this round the cast to form a second loop.
2. Twist the loop round the cast again and then pull the knot tight and cut off the loose end.

45 The Two-turn Turle Knot

Two-turn turle (Fig. 45). This is for attaching a cast to a hook, or fly.

1. Pass the end of the cast through the eye of the hook.
2. Push the hook up the cast out of the way.
3. Twist the free end of the cast round the shaft of the cast to form a loop.
4. Twist the free end twice round the loop.
5. Pull the free end of the cast until the knot is tight.
6. Push the hook through the loop, then pull on the cast until the knot is held tightly round the shank of the hook and against the eye.

Chapter 23

BITS AND PIECES

IN THIS final chapter there will be found many little things which directly, or indirectly, concern the angler. First of all, I think, one should refer to the question of the child angler. I am now presuming that the angler is competent enough to pass on his knowledge to the young idea.

This passing on of knowledge to a youngster is the finest way of retaining enthusiasm for the sport.

Teaching a youngster prevents one becoming blasé, and also brings about a rich and pleasant relationship between adult and child.

Irrespective of the age of the child there are certain things which must be borne in mind by the teacher. In the first place, if you take a youngster fishing with you, DO NOT EXPECT TO DO MUCH ANGLING YOURSELF.

Most of the time will be spent in setting up, or helping to set up tackle, untangling lines, watching to see that the child does not get into a dangerous situation, as well as extracting hooks from clothing, and so on. Again, you must not expect a healthy, normal child to be content with the type of fishing you want to do. There is little patience in the average child and it is too much to expect him (or her) to sit it out waiting for a bite for any period longer than about 30 minutes without success.

On the other hand, if the angler *is* getting fish, then it will become practically impossible to persuade the child to call it quits when the time comes to go home.

Youngsters can become anglers at almost any age. My own son started at two and a half years and now catches fish on many occasions when I have been without a bite! But there are certain definite rules to be kept. Keep the instruction interesting. Safety discipline, whether ashore or afloat, must be well indoctrinated, in an interesting and palatable manner well before the child makes his first fishing trip.

If one is going afloat – then take only one youngster. It is difficult to control children in a boat and if you should have a couple of them to look after and instruct, it is surprising how the other will get into trouble the moment you are fully engaged with the one!

I would advocate, also, that where possible the children should be able to swim. But as this state of affairs is not always possible then you, as their instructor, and guardian, must be able to do so. It is most unfair and selfish, even downright cowardly, to take sport beside or on water if one cannot swim and this offence is aggravated if young people are in that person's care.

But angling with a youngster helps one to relive and revive the past. During the angling, as well as before and after, you can pass on to them the secrets of nature. How a fish breathes, the different kinds of bait, and, best of all, how to get the bait, and get them to help you with this.

Sea angling teachers will find that bait digging soon becomes a grand frolic and part of the fun of angling!

Children soon take to fishing. There are so many attractions to it. Getting out tackle before a trip, the actual journey, and, of course, spending the day with Dad or Uncle *as a pal*, are all part of the day. Fishing to a child in particular consists of lots of little important items in one day, not merely wetting the line. But all the same, the youngster must be prepared for fishless days and that possibility should be anticipated.

DO NOT, ABOVE EVERYTHING ELSE, EQUIP A YOUNGSTER WITH CAST-OFF ANGLING MATERIAL. Let the child have his own rod and reel, suited to his needs. It may only be a cheap little rod, but it will be his own. In any case it is not fair to expect a child to handle your own old equipment and expect him to do well with it.

In addition to natural history lessons, particularly during the inevitable slack periods, imbue them with a knowledge of weather lore, country code, tide times, river currents, and talk to them about the different kinds of angling waters.

And, above all, teach them the principles of conservation and the ideals of good sportsmanship. If you can manage it, get out with them to various aquaria where they can see the fish swimming and feeding. Even a tropical tank at home, which need not cost very much, will keep them interested and it is surprising what they will learn from such a source.

So why not take a youngster along with you on one of your trips? He'll be no bother, and believe me, you will gain a lot from such an outing. Mutual respect and good companionship between man and boy, a reawakening of youthful enthusiasm in the breast of the older angler, and a constant reappraisal of angling values will all flow from such an angling partnership.

Above all, angling, taught properly, is an excellent form of character building for a child. Patience, good sportsmanship, a true appreciation of outdoor life and creatures can be bestowed by you on that youngster. I think my own proudest moments come when my own youngster lands his fish : his triumph is also mine. But remember, the child must be started properly and the teacher must be prepared to sacrifice some of his own angling to see that the child gets his. It's worth it – try it.

*　　　*　　　*

The angler, as he progresses, will find that there are various societies and organizations given over to the interests of angling. I think that the list below should provide most anglers with an opportunity of finding the body best suited to their needs and I have purposely omitted the addresses of the societies concerned. Today, with rebuilding going on over all the country, addresses are continually changing. If the angler wishes to contact any of the bodies in question his best plan is to write to his own angling paper *enclosing a stamped addressed envelope* and asking for the name and address of the secretary.

The principal societies of interest to the angler are:

Anglers Co-operative Association – this very important body fights pollution of our waters and it is recommended anglers give it every assistance possible.

British Casting Association – organizes casting tournaments which are a form of angling game.

British Conger Club – for those interested in catching specimen conger in British waters.

British Field Sports Society – for all field sports including angling interests.

British Record (Rod Caught) Fish Committee, which investigates and recommends and maintains a register of record rod-caught fish both freshwater and sea fish.

National Federation of Anglers – coarse fishing competitions.

National Federation of Sea Anglers – mostly competitions for sea angling clubs.

Pure Rivers Society – interested in keeping waters unpolluted.

Salmon and Trout Association – as its name implies.

Flyfishers Club – as this title indicates.

Shark Angling Club of Great Britain – the body which looks after shark angling in British waters.

*   *   *

Half of the fun of angling consists in keeping an angling diary. Not a dry-as-dust record of days out, but a lively document which records dates and places visited, baits used, weather conditions, species caught (or not caught), and so on. Each entry should tell a complete story: for example it should not contain entries like:

'Aug. 30. River Mole. 2 chub.'

rather the entry would read:

'Aug. 30. Sunday. R. Mole at . . . Fished from the high

bank below the bridge. Wind gentle. Water, rather low. Sky clear but tending to cloud over as day progressed. Bait used – chub fly, allowed to dap on the surface. No luck. Changed to cheese. No luck. Finally changed back to dapping again and two chub within ten minutes. Weight. . . . Rod used. . . .'

Finally, without apology, I close this book with the following tips as well as general observations on angler etiquette and conduct :

1. Always make certain that your reel is securely attached to your rod before fishing.

2. If your reel does come off (assuming it does not fall into the water) do not attempt to replace the reel on the rod while playing the fish. Use the line and the rod. You can unravel the tangle at your feet after the fish has been landed !

3. Wherever possible carry a spear fitting for your rod so that it may be placed in the ground to stand upright. This prevents damage to the rod, often caused through the silly practice of laying a rod on the ground.

4. When fishing from a boat do not leave the rod unattended. Unattended rods go overboard through one cause or another.

5. If you have to carry a rod, fully assembled, along the river bank and have to pass through woods, bushes, or so on, carry it butt first. This prevents the rod tip being broken should you stumble when carrying it.

6. Close all gates behind you.

7. Do not leave litter, discarded hooks, broken casts, cigarette cartons, bottles, at the waterside.

8. Do not throw litter and other material into the water.

9. Do not carry portable transistor radios with you and play them at the waterside, a common Thames-side practice I am afraid !

10. If you are taking part in a coarse fishing match try to stop your companions doing things which might lead

219

to complaints about your club or party. Banging of car and coach doors in late evening or early morning, the use of bad language, should be curbed as much as possible. If necessary do not hesitate to report an offender to the club committee – basically anglers are decent chaps and this sort of conduct has cost coarse fishers a lot of angling water in recent years.

11. When fishing from a boat do not row across the drift of another. ·

12. In passing another angler at the waterside make a detour so that you will neither disturb him nor the fish.

13. Let fly fishers on a river have preference : they are moving along the water and soon pass out of your way.

14. If requested by a fellow angler, give him truthfully the information he asks.

15. If going to fish in areas where there are likely to be swarms of midges, take a repellent with you. This applies particularly to Scotland, and also to marshy districts.

Finally, remember that you, yourself, at the waterside are an ambassador of fishing. What you do will be judged by non-anglers as conduct typical of all anglers. For example, one day at Walton-on-Thames I heard a splash and saw a small child, a toddler, fall into the river. I ran from the bridge on which I was standing, to the path to go to its rescue, but before I reached the spot a young woman had dived in and brought the child out. During the whole of this time two young men anglers had sat there watching the whole thing and the only thing one of them could say was 'They've ruined this swim.' Can you imagine what that young woman thought about anglers from then on? On the other hand, many an angler has risked his own life to save a person from drowning.

*　　　*　　　*

In the foregoing chapters I hope that I have introduced

the reader to angling in some of its various forms, and I would like to think that I have been of assistance in some way to him. 'Tight lines' is an angling expression, by which one angler wishes the other good luck. And 'tight lines' is exactly what I wish each and every reader.

Appendix

APPENDIX

RIVER AUTHORITIES

THE AUTHORITIES listed below were created under the Water Resources Act 1963, replacing the River Boards which previously existed:

Avon & Dorset: Rostherene, 3 St Stephen's Road, Bournemouth, Hants.

Bristol Avon: Green Park Road, Bath, Somerset.

Cornwall: St Johns, Western Road, Launceston, Cornwall.

Cumberland: 256 London Road, Carlisle, Cumberland.

Dee and Clwyd: 2 Vicar's Lane, Chester.

Devon: County Hall, Exeter.

East Suffolk and Norfolk: The Cedars, Albemarle Road, Norwich.

Essex: Rivers House, 129 Springfield Road, Chelmsford, Essex.

Glamorgan: Tremaine House, Coychurch Road, Bridgend, Glamorgan.

Great Ouse: Elmhurst, Brooklands Avenue, Cambridge.

Gwynedd: Highfield, Caernarvon.

Hampshire: The Castle, Winchester, Hants.

Isle of Wight: County Hall, Newport, Isle of Wight.

Kent: Rivers House, London Road, Maidstone, Kent.

Lancashire: 48 West Cliff, Preston, Lancashire.

Lincolnshire: 50 Wide Bargate, Boston, Lincs.

Mersey and Weaver: Liverpool Road, Great Sankey, Warrington, Lancs.

Northumbrian: Dunira, 110 Osborne Road, Newcastle-upon-Tyne.

Severn: Portland House, Church Street, Great Malvern, Worcs.

Somerset: 12 King Square, Bridgwater, Somerset.

South-west Wales: Penyfai House, Penyfai Lane, Llanelly.

Sussex: 51 Church Road, Burgess Hill, Sussex.

Trent: 206 Derby Road, Nottingham.

Usk: The Croft, Goldcroft Common, Caerleon, Newport, Monmouthshire.

Welland and Nene: North Street, Oundle, Nr. Peterborough.

Wye: 4 St John Street, Hereford.

Yorkshire Ouse and Hull: 21 Park Square South, Leeds, 1.

CATCHMENT BOARDS

Lee Conservancy: Brettenham House, Lancaster Place, Strand, London, W. C. 2.

River Thames above Teddington Lock: Thames Conservancy, Burdett House, 15 Buckingham Street, London, W. C. 2.

INDEX

228

229

GIPSY MOTH
CIRCLES THE WORLD
Illustrated 6/-
FRANCIS CHICHESTER

'Sir Francis's own story of one of
the great adventures of modern times…
he is as neat with his pen as he is
nifty with his navigation'—
Daily Mirror

MY LIVELY LADY
Illustrated 6/-
ALEC ROSE

'A lively tale of a lively voyage'
The Evening News
'One of the most descriptive pieces
of yachting writing to have been
published for a decade'
Yachting and Boating Weekly
'A vivid and good-humoured chronicle'
The Daily Telegraph

COLES NOTES FOR STUDENTS

Coles Notes are a comprehensive range of study aids especially designed to help the students of G.C.E. 'O' and 'A' level examinations. Each Note in the English Literature series gives a detailed synopsis of the story and analysis of the character and the character development. In the case of Science, History, Geography and Language titles, the subject matter is covered clearly and concisely and will form an ideal companion to your school books.

Shakespeare

ANTHONY AND CLEOPATRA	7/6
CORIOLANUS	8/–
HAMLET	7/6
JULIUS CAESAR	7/6
KING LEAR	7/6
KING HENRY V	7/6
MACBETH	7/6
THE MERCHANT OF VENICE	7/6
A MIDSUMMER NIGHT'S DREAM	7/6
MUCH ADO ABOUT NOTHING	8/–
OTHELLO	7/6
RICHARD II	8/–
RICHARD III	7/6
ROMEO AND JULIET	7/6
THE TAMING OF THE SHREW	7/6
THE TEMPEST	7/6
TROILUS AND CRESSIDA	8/–
TWELFTH NIGHT	7/6
THE WINTER'S TALE	7/6

Shakespeare Total Study editions available for most plays

Chaucer, Total Study Edition

PROLOGUE TO THE CANTERBURY TALES	10/6
WIFE OF BATH'S TALE	10/–

Chaucer

THE NUN'S PRIEST'S TALE	7/6
THE PARDONER'S TALE	7/6
THE CLERK'S TALE	7/6
THE PRIORESS'S TALE	8/–
THE PROLOGUE TO THE CANTERBURY TALES	7/6
THE CANTERBURY TALES	7/6

Literature

EMMA Jane Austen	7/6
NORTHANGER ABBEY Jane Austen	7/6
PERSUASION Jane Austen	7/6
PRIDE AND PREJUDICE Jane Austen	7/6
LORNA DOONE R. D. Blackmore	7/6
JANE EYRE Charlotte Bronte	7/6
WUTHERING HEIGHTS Emily Bronte	7/6
THE PLAGUE Albert Camus	7/6
THE STRANGER Albert Camus	8/–
HEART OF DARKNESS Joseph Conrad	8/–
LORD JIM Joseph Conrad	8/–
GREAT EXPECTATIONS Charles Dickens	7/6
A TALE OF TWO CITIES Charles Dickens	7/6
ADAM BEDE George Eliot	7/6
THE MILL ON THE FLOSS George Eliot	7/6
MIDDLEMARCH George Eliot	8/–
SILAS MARNER George Eliot	7/6
TOM JONES Henry Fielding	7/6
GREAT GATSBY F. Scott Fitzgerald	7/6
MADAME BOVARY Flaubert	8/–
THE GUN C. S. Forester	8/–
A PASSAGE TO INDIA E. M. Forster	7/6
LORD OF THE FLIES William Golding	7/6
THE VICAR OF WAKEFIELD Oliver Goldsmith	7/6
THE POWER AND THE GLORY Graham Greene	8/–
FAR FROM THE MADDING CROWD Thomas Hardy	7/6
THE MAYOR OF CASTERBRIDGE Thomas Hardy	7/6
FOR WHOM THE BELL TOLLS, FAREWELL TO ARMS	
Ernest Hemingway	7/6
THE OLD MAN AND THE SEA Ernest Hemingway	7/6
THE SUN ALSO RISES Ernest Hemingway	7/6
BRAVE NEW WORLD Aldous Huxley	8/–
PORTRAIT OF THE ARTIST AS A YOUNG MAN	
James Joyce	7/6
KIM Rudyard Kipling	7/6
SONS AND LOVERS D. H. Lawrence	7/6
BABBIT, MAIN STREET Sinclair Lewis	8/–
MOBY DICK Herman Melville	7/6
ANIMAL FARM George Orwell	7/6
1984 George Orwell	7/6
THE GRAPES OF WRATH John Steinbeck	7/6
THE PEARL John Steinbeck	7/6
GULLIVER'S TRAVELS Jonathan Swift	7/6
VANITY FAIR William Thackeray	7/6
THE ADVENTURES OF HUCKLEBERRY FINN	
Mark Twain	7/6

Also available now our new series called
Forum House which is specially prepared for
the University Student.

MAJOR BRITISH ROMANTIC POETS	20/–
G. B. SHAW—CREATIVE ARTIST	15/–
MODERN ENGLISH POETS	10/–
D. H. LAWRENCE: A CRITICAL SURVEY	20/–
WRITERS OF THE ROMANTIC PERIOD	12/6

The Man and His Works

SAMUEL BECKETT edited by Frederick Hoffman	15/–
T. S. ELIOT Eric Thompson	15/–
E. M. FORSTER Norman Kelvin	15/–
F. SCOTT FITZGERALD Richard D. Lehan	15/–
CHRISTOPHER FRY Emil Roy	15/–
JAMES JOYCE Joseph Prescott	15/–
D. H. LAWRENCE Harry T. Moore	20/–
HENRY MILLER edited by George Wickes	15/–
EUGENE O'NEILL John Henry Raleigh	20/–

History of English Literature Series

ANGLO-SAXON AND MIDDLE ENGLISH LITERATURE	8/–
RENAISSANCE PROSE AND POETRY	8/–
CONTEMPORARY AMERICAN NOVELISTS	15/–
CONTEMPORARY BRITISH NOVELISTS	15/–
CONTEMPORARY EUROPEAN NOVELISTS	15/–

The Man and His Plays

SEAN O'CASEY Jules Koslow	8/–

Notes on General Anthropology

PRE-HISTORY AND CULTURAL GROWTH	10/–
CULTURAL PATTERNS AND DYNAMICS	10/–
AN OUTLINE HISTORY OF PHILOSOPHY	12/–
NOTES ON BASIC POLITICAL THEORY	15/–

General Reference Titles

HOW TO USE THE SLIDE RULE	8/6
DEVELOP YOUR SPEED READING POWER	8/6
DICTIONARY OF SYNONYMS AND ANTONYMS WITH DISCRIMINATIONS	15/–

ANDY CAPP

=MAN OF THE HOUR

A FAWCETT GOLD MEDAL BOOK

Fawcett Publications, Inc., Greenwich, Conn.
Member of American Book Publishers Council, Inc.

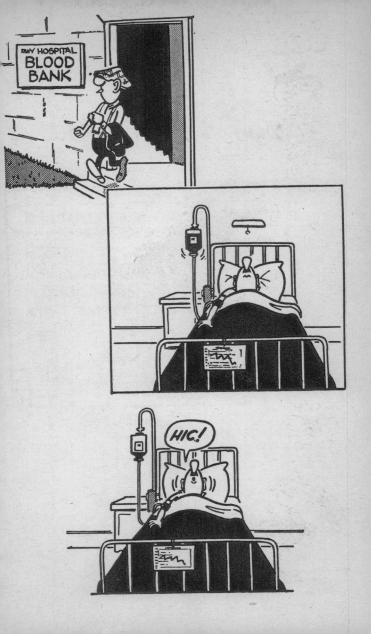

WHAT'S THE USE! I TALK ME 'EAD OFF, BUT IT ALWAYS ENDS UP WITH 'IM SAYING 'LET'S DRINK T' THAT'!

CAR SHOWROOM

HEY, PET, I WAS JUST THINKIN' – 'OW ABOUT US SAVIN' UP FOR A CAR?

WOULDN'T IT BE SIMPLER TO MOVE TO A HOUSE NEARER TO THE PUB?

IF THERE'S ANYTHIN' WORSE THAN A WIFE WHO DOESN'T UNDERSTAND YER, IT'S ONE WHO DOES

Smythe

LET THAT BE A LESSON T' YER!

TCH! I'LL POP OVER AN' GET A COUPLE OF ASPRINS F' YER, PET

OOOW! ME 'EAD!

ISN'T 'E SWEET?

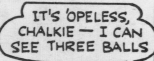

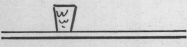

DOWN A BIT—A SHADE T' YER LEFT—A BIT MORE... GO ON— WHOA! THAT'S IT

AND THAT'S ONLY THE WEATHER FORECAST!

Smythe

IT'S SCANDALOUS! THE REST O' THE BLOKES IN THE STREET OUT WORKIN' —AN' YOU KICKIN' A BALL ABOUT ENJOYIN' YERSELF!

I KNOW, PET, I'VE TRIED TALKIN' T' THEM, BUT THEY DON'T TAKE A BLIND BIT O' NOTICE

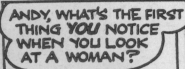

C'MON, CHEER UP! WE MIGHT BE A BIT 'ARD UP – BUT THERE'S 'EAPS O' WOMEN WORSE OFF THAN YOU ARE, PET

NAME ONE!

WHAT D'YER FANCY IN THE THIRD?